OPEN MARXISM

VS.

SECTARIAN DOGMA

Defending Ernest Mandel Against the
Alliance for Workers' Liberty

Red Mole

Folrose Press, London

ISBN: 978-0-906378-21-2 print

ISBN: 978-0-906378-22-9 ebook

TABLE OF CONTENTS

Part One

Ernest Mandel's Theoretical Legacy

Ernest Mandel's Evolving Perspectives on 20th Century Socialism and Capitalism

I. Introduction: Ernest Mandel – A Leading Marxist Thinker of the 20th Century

Ernest Mandel (1923-1995) stands as a towering figure in 20th-century Marxist thought, renowned for his rigorous economic analysis, unwavering political commitment, and prolific writings translated into over 40 languages. Born in Frankfurt am Main to Jewish emigres from Poland with deep left-wing sympathies, the tumultuous events of his youth profoundly shaped Mandel's intellectual and political trajectory. His father, Henri Mandel, was drawn to Leon Trotsky's ideas, and their Antwerp home became a refuge for left-wing exiles fleeing Nazi Germany in the 1930s. This early exposure to anti-Stalinist radicalism and the horrors of fascism instilled in Mandel a lifelong dedication to the struggle against capitalism, a system he viewed as inherently generating such barbarism.

During World War II, Mandel actively participated in the Belgian resistance, enduring imprisonment and forced labor in Nazi camps. His survival, despite being a Jew and a Trotskyist despised by Stalinist fellow prisoners, solidified his resolve to dismantle the capitalist system. This period remained a critical political and moral reference point throughout his life. Postwar, Mandel emerged as a leading voice in the global Trotskyist movement, serving as a founder and editor of the Belgian left socialist weekly *La Gauche* and contributing extensively to economic and political journals worldwide.

His outspoken critique of both capitalism and bureaucratic "socialist" states led to him being barred from numerous countries, including the United States and West Germany, where he was deported to prevent a university appointment.

Mandel's theoretical framework was anchored in a steadfast commitment to Trotskyism, consistently developing and applying Leon Trotsky's insights throughout his career, exemplified by works such as *Trotsky as Alternative*. Central to his analytical approach was the meticulous application of the Marxist dialectical method. He conceptualized social phenomena not in isolation but as interconnected totalities, emphasizing the "unity in contradiction of relations and process". This allowed him to analyze social reality as a dynamic interplay of opposing forces, constantly evolving and characterized by inherent tensions. His historical materialism insisted on a class-determined analysis grounded in real-world material conditions.

Given the complexity and often contentious nature of Mandel's positions, particularly within the fragmented landscape of 20th-century Marxist thought, descriptions of his views are frequently unreliable. This report aims to counter such inaccuracies by meticulously drawing from his extensive bibliography and authoritative secondary sources, providing precise citations and contextual analysis to ensure an accurate and nuanced portrayal of his evolving theoretical and political contributions.

II. The Evolution of Mandel's Theoretical Positions: A Dynamic Marxism

Ernest Mandel's intellectual journey was marked by a continuous process of theoretical development and refinement, reflecting his commitment to a living, empirically responsive Marxism. His prolific output spanned decades, addressing the most pressing economic and political questions of his time.

His engagement with post-war socialist experiments began early, with works such as *Nature and Perspectives of the China of Mao Tse-Tung* (1951), *The Theory of "State Capitalism"* (1951), and *First Balance Sheet of the Yugoslav Affair* (1952). These early analyses demonstrated his immediate critical engagement with the emerging "socialist" states. His foundational economic work,

Marxist Economic Theory, published in 1962, provided a comprehensive exposition of his understanding of Marx's economic doctrine, followed by a more concise *An Introduction to Marxist Economic Theory* in 1967.

In the 1960s, Mandel developed the concept of "neo-capitalism" to characterize the post-World War II capitalist era, which saw unprecedented growth, technological innovation, and increased state intervention. He later refined this concept to "late capitalism," the title of his seminal work published in 1975. This theoretical shift aimed to capture the essence of this new phase, emphasizing that while capitalism's fundamental nature remained

unchanged, its concrete forms and dynamics had evolved. His work on *Long Waves of Capitalist Development* (1995) further elaborated his understanding of capitalism's inherent, cyclical dynamics, linking these long waves to the system's internal contradictions. Later in his career, he continued to produce significant theoretical works, including *From Stalinism to Eurocommunism: The Bitter Fruits of 'Socialism in One Country'* (1978) and *Power and Money: A Marxist Theory of Bureaucracy* (1992), which reflected his ongoing critical engagement with the nature of bureaucratic states and the enduring legacy of Stalinism.

Mandel's intellectual integrity was evident in his capacity for self-criticism and theoretical revision. In *Late Capitalism*, he critically assessed his earlier *Marxist Economic Theory*, noting its "exaggeratedly descriptive character" and a "too small effort to explain the contemporary history of capitalism by its immanent laws of motion". This self-assessment indicated a deliberate shift in his analytical focus towards a more explanatory and dynamically driven theoretical approach in his subsequent economic analyses. This refinement was not a mere change of mind but a conscious effort to make Marxist categories more robust and empirically grounded, capable of explaining the concrete historical processes of capitalism. This dynamic approach, where theory is refined in dialogue with observed reality, distinguished him from more dogmatic Marxist tendencies.

A notable instance of this responsiveness to empirical observation was his revision concerning economic stagnation. His earlier, incorrect adherence to the idea of an "irreversible stagnation of the economy shortly after the Second World War" directly led to his later development of the "long wave" theory. This intellectual journey convinced him of the necessity of studying a third type of economic rhythm, beyond short-term industrial cycles and the system's overall life cycle, to fully grasp capitalism's complex dynamics. This commitment to adapting and deepening Marxist theory in response to new empirical data underscores his view of Marxism as a living science, rather than a static dogma.

The following provides a chronological overview of the evolution of Mandel's views on key topics, highlighting the shifts and continuities in his thought.

Evolution of Mandel's Views on Key Topics

China (Maoism)

- ◆ 1951 (*Nature and Perspectives of the China of Mao Tse-Tung*): Initial analysis of the revolution's nature.
- ◆ 1967 (*The Cultural Revolution – An Attempt at Interpretation*): Detailed critique of agricultural errors, social differentiation, and the Cultural Revolution as an inter-bureaucratic struggle.

Shift from general analysis to specific, nuanced critique of Maoist economic policies and the bureaucratic nature of the Cultural Revolution, emphasizing internal contradictions and mass reawakening.

USSR (Nature of State)

- ◆ **1951** (*The Theory of "State Capitalism"*): Early engagement with the debate, rejecting "state capitalism".
- ◆ **1981** (*The Laws of Motion of the Soviet Economy*): Developed concept of "transitional society" (deformed workers' state) as neither capitalist nor socialist, driven by bureaucratic consumption privileges rather than profit.

Consistent rejection of "state capitalism" but deepened the theoretical framework for understanding the unique, non-capitalist, yet non-socialist, nature of the Soviet economy and its internal contradictions.

Yugoslavia (Market Socialism)

- ◆ **1952** (*First Balance Sheet of the Yugoslav Affair*): Early assessment of the post-split Yugoslav experiment.
- ◆ **1967** (*Yugoslav Economic Theory*): Detailed critique of market mechanisms leading to inequality and the persistence of bureaucracy, despite self-management rhetoric.

Evolution from initial observation to a comprehensive critique, arguing that market mechanisms, even with self-management, exacerbate inequality and do not resolve bureaucratic control, merely shifting its form.

"Socialism in One Country"

- ◆ **1950s-60s:** Consistent opposition, rooted in Trotsky's Permanent Revolution theory.

- **1978** (*From Stalinism to Euro-communism*),
- **1989** (*Beyond Perestroika*): Reaffirmed that isolated socialist construction is impossible; the international context is decisive.

Unwavering opposition to the theory, consistently arguing for the international nature of socialist victory and the inherent fragility and bureaucratic deformation of isolated post-capitalist states.

Democratic Rights Under Socialism

- **1950s-60s:** Implicit in Trotskyist critique of Stalinism.
- **1970s-80s:** Explicit advocacy for unlimited political democracy, multi-party systems, and full press freedom as essential for genuine socialism.

Developed a more explicit and detailed program for socialist democracy, emphasizing its functional necessity for economic rationality and the self-emancipation of the working class, directly contrasting with bureaucratic regimes.

Capitalist Development

- **1960s** (e.g., *The Economics of Neo-Capitalism*): Developed concept of "neo-capitalism".
- **1975** (*Late Capitalism*), **1995** (*Long Waves of Capitalist Development*): Refined "neo-capitalism" to "late capitalism"; developed "long wave" theory, incorporating self-criticism on earlier stagnation predictions.

Shift from describing post-war capitalism to providing a deeper theoretical explanation of its internal dynamics and cyclical patterns, acknowledging and correcting earlier analytical limitations.

III. Mandel's Analysis of Maoism and the Chinese Revolution

Ernest Mandel approached the Chinese Revolution and Maoism with a nuanced, critical Marxist lens, rejecting simplistic interpretations and insisting on a rigorous analytical effort to discern their objective meaning. He viewed the "cultural revolution" as the "most complex phenomenon faced by revolutionary Marxists in recent decades".

Initial Views and Critiques of Mao's Agricultural Policies and the Cultural Revolution

Mandel critically assessed the Maoist leadership's agricultural policies, particularly their "overestimation of the capacity of the peasantry to make sacrifices in order to industrialize the country rapidly". These errors, he noted, led to "serious setbacks suffered by Chinese agriculture and economy during the 1959-61 period," necessitating a considerable slowdown in the rate of economic growth, despite subsequent rehabilitation efforts.

He observed a significant "social differentiation" emerging in Chinese villages following the "rectification" of the "great leap forward" excesses. This was evidenced by disparities in crop yields and incomes between "working teams" based on former rich peasant households and those based on poor peasants, as well as interregional differences where communes near urban centers specialized in more profitable produce, yielding higher incomes than grain-producing areas. This indicated a divergence from official egalitarian narratives. Mandel also highlighted the underlying tension between the peasantry and the state, stemming from the state's siphoning off a considerable portion of the agricultural surplus for industrial investments, often with fluctuating prices for agricultural products. He noted the accusations against Liu Shao-chi for advocating policies that would increase private plots and market production, suggesting fundamental differences on the agricultural question.

Mandel analyzed the Red Guard movement as a deliberate appeal by Mao to the masses, bypassing party and state cadres, when he faced internal opposition. While Mao initially focused on student youth, who were perceived as easier to indoctrinate and less disruptive to industrial production, Mandel observed that Mao underestimated the "explosive nature" of the themes introduced and the "rapid resurrection of a critical spirit" among the mobilized masses. This led to thousands of young people questioning the entire bureaucracy, including the Maoist faction. The "turn of January 1967" saw the Maoist faction forced to modify its approach, resorting to repression against nonconformist Red Guards and pro-Liu Shaochi groups, ultimately leading to a re-alliance with a majority of the bureaucracy, with the army intervening to seal the "triple alliance for seizing power". Mandel cited examples of independent worker action, such as the "General National Rebel Corps of Red Workers" demonstrating for back wages, illustrating that mass mobilization could develop its own momentum beyond the control of the Maoist leadership.

Analysis of Bureaucratic Methods and the Class Character of the Chinese State

Mandel argued that the systematic organization of the "Mao cult" did not signify a progressive abolition of soviet or internal party democracy, as these had never fully existed in China after the 1949 victory. Instead, it served the needs of "inter-bureaucratic struggles". He contrasted this with Stalin's rise, which involved the progressive consolidation of bureaucratic power facilitated by the complete political passivity of the masses. In China, Mandel identified a "weakening of the bureaucracy" and a "reawakening of the masses," particularly due to the shattering of its monolithic unity. This observation suggests that even bureaucratically initiated movements can generate popular agency that is difficult to contain. The subsequent need for the "triple alliance" and military intervention to reassert control illustrates the inherent instability of bureaucratic rule when confronted with genuinely mobilized popular forces, highlighting the bureaucracy's ultimate reliance on coercion rather than democratic legitimacy.

He criticized the "triple alliance" for bringing "hardened bureaucrats to power everywhere" and lamented the near absence of genuine workers' councils or soviet-type organs in factories, with the Shanghai glassworks being a rare, quickly abandoned exception. Mandel found Mao's attribution of the revolution's degeneration primarily to ideological factors, rather than the material infrastructure of society or inadequate development of productive forces, to be "absolutely foreign to Marxism". He argued that Mao substituted a subjective "sociology," defining "capitalist" as anyone disagreeing with "Mao Tse-tung's thought," for a Marxist, objective analysis. This substitution of an "imaginary" danger of "capitalist restoration" for actual bureaucratic degeneration led to remedies, such as suppressing dissent, that ultimately reinforced the degeneration. He asserted that the Chinese revolution, from its inception, was a "deformed revolution" where the proletariat played only a contributory role, and a peasant army replaced independent mass action. The party itself bore a "heavy Stalinist imprint" from the start.

Mandel's Perspective on the Sino-Soviet Split and its Implications for China

Mandel attributed the Sino-Soviet split to the Kremlin's increasingly "conservative course," characterized by "peaceful coexistence" and "economic competition," driven by a fear of the "increasing scale and independence of the new revolutionary forces" globally. The immediate causes of the break included the Soviet bureaucracy's refusal to provide nuclear weapons or aid in their manufacture to China, coupled with an abrupt cessation of economic aid.

He placed "chief responsibility for the political crisis now raging in China" squarely on the Soviet bureaucracy, citing its "sabotage of economic aid and the subsequent economic blockade of China," and its "failure to reply adequately to imperialist aggression" in Vietnam. While acknowledging the Maoist leaders' "share of responsibility" for their "ultra-opportunistic policies" towards the Indonesian government and Communist Party (which prevented a revolutionary victory) and their "sectarianism on the united front in defense of the Vietnamese revolution," he maintained that these errors did not obscure the main source of the Chinese crisis.

This analysis of the Sino-Soviet split provides a crucial understanding of the limitations of "socialism in one country" models, even those Mandel viewed as "deformed workers' states." The Soviet Union's actions, such as withdrawing aid and refusing nuclear technology, demonstrate that even states that have formally "overthrown capitalism" are subject to national interests and geopolitical pressures that can lead to inter-state conflicts, undermining solidarity and development in other "socialist" countries. This reinforces the broader argument that the success of socialist construction is ultimately dependent on the international context and cannot be fully secured within isolated national borders, particularly when the primary threat comes from a "fellow" bureaucratic regime rather than direct capitalist encirclement. This highlights the inherent contradictions and instability of isolated revolutionary processes.

Later Views on China's Economic Crisis and Political Repression

In his 1982 "Post Scriptum" on China, Mandel detailed the country's economic policies of readjustment, retrenchment, and austerity throughout 1981, noting a significant fall in economic growth and rampant inflation due to cumulative budget deficits. He observed a substantial expansion of the private sector in agriculture, services, and retail, including the authorization for private businessmen to hire wage-earners, a clear departure from earlier collectivization efforts and a move towards market-oriented reforms. The "loosening of the 'right to work' rule" led to pay cuts, dismissals, and a significant rise in urban unemployment (estimated at ten million), indicating the reintroduction of market-based labor discipline.

Mandel explicitly connected these economic developments to the Deng faction's rapid curbing of "modest political 'liberalisation'" and a "sharpening repression". This observation reveals a critical causal relationship: the introduction of market-oriented economic reforms, which generated increased social tensions and worker protests, necessitated a tightening of political control to manage these emergent contradictions and prevent them from escalating into challenges to the bureaucracy's political monopoly. This suggests that for bureaucratic states, economic liberalization, particularly when it introduces inequality and insecurity, often requires a suppression of political freedoms, as the inherent contradictions of such a hybrid system cannot be resolved democratically without threatening the bureaucracy's material privileges and political power.

IV. Cuba and Castroism: A Critical Embrace

Ernest Mandel's engagement with the Cuban Revolution was characterized by an initial enthusiastic embrace of its social achievements, followed by a nuanced critical analysis of its economic model and the persistent challenges of bureaucratic deformation.

Initial Support and Admiration for the Cuban Revolution's Social Achievements

Mandel's initial views and support for the Cuban Revolution were overwhelmingly positive and enthusiastic, particularly after his seven-week visit in 1964. He lauded the revolution's profound social transformations, such as converting barracks into schools, repurposing luxurious mansions for scholarship students, and educating a million adolescents and adults.

Mandel praised the radical suppression of racial inequality and segregation, and the "miracle of eliminating, in three years, unemployment and underemployment in the rural areas – a notorious evil in all underdeveloped economies". He was impressed by the Rebel Army's egalitarian structure, which eliminated ranks above commandant, and noted the dedication of ministers and officials performing guard duty as ordinary militiamen.

Mandel viewed Cuba as "the most advanced bastion of the emancipation of man," showcasing "the immense possibilities of radical social change, of human liberation, that socialism offers the human race".

Nuanced Views on Cuba's Economic Model, Particularly Debates with Che Guevara on the Law of Value and Central Planning

Mandel visited Cuba in 1964 and again in 1967, actively participating in the "Great Economic Debate" within the Cuban leadership. He notably sided with Che Guevara against those advocating for Soviet-style market mechanisms and the direct application of the law of value. He critically argued that relying on the "law of value" to directly regulate production in underdeveloped countries would inevitably lead to the reproduction of underdevelopment, as it would prioritize immediate profitability over necessary long-term economic and social development, such as industrialization.

Mandel distinguished between "violating the law of value" (which could lead to economic losses if done blindly) and "disregarding it" (which was necessary for a planned, socialist transformation in underdeveloped contexts, particularly through the monopoly of foreign trade). He emphasized the need for strict calculation of real production costs and a stable monetary yardstick, allowing the law of value to guide only sectors where economic or social priorities did not dictate otherwise. This deep engagement with the Cuban economic debate reveals a crucial understanding of the challenges of socialist construction in underdeveloped countries. It suggests that the mere abolition of private ownership is insufficient; the "law of value" (market logic) can still reassert itself and perpetuate underdevelopment if not consciously "violated" or "disregarded" by central planning. This implies that for genuine socialist transformation in the Global South, political and social priorities must actively override immediate economic "profitability" as defined by capitalist metrics. His alignment with Che Guevara on this point underscores a shared understanding of the need for a non-market, planned path to overcome historical underdevelopment, directly connecting to his broader critique of "socialism in one country" if it meant susceptibility to world market pressures.

He strongly supported financing enterprises through the State budget, especially for large industries, aligning with Che Guevara's Budgetary Finance System (BFS) as opposed to self-financing and bank loans.

Concerns about Bureaucratic Deformation and the Importance of Workers' Democracy

Mandel consistently warned against the dangers of excessive autonomy for enterprises, particularly in underdeveloped countries. He argued that if self-management units retained large investment funds, they would tend to prioritize local or sectoral interests over national ones, leading to increased inequality and hindering national industrialization goals. He contended that the primary danger of bureaucracy did not reside in centralization itself, but in the "absence of workers' democracy at the national political level". He frequently quoted Trotsky, emphasizing that "only the co-ordination of three elements, state planning, the market and Soviet democracy, can assure correct guidance of the economy of the epoch of transition".

Mandel advocated for genuine workers' management at the enterprise level and robust workers' democracy at the state level (e.g., through a national congress of workers' councils) as essential safeguards against bureaucratization. He actively sought to persuade Cuban leaders, including Che Guevara, of the critical importance of building socialist democracy. This consistent and strong emphasis on workers' democracy as the fundamental safeguard against bureaucratic deformation, even in the context of a revolutionary state like Cuba, represents a core principle of his Marxist thought. This extends beyond specific economic debates to a universal requirement for any genuine socialist transition. His argument that "centralization itself" is not the problem, but rather the *lack of democratic control over it*, is a crucial nuance. This implies that even if economic policies are theoretically sound and aimed at socialist goals, without robust democratic accountability and participation from below, bureaucratic interests will inevitably distort the revolutionary project, leading to inefficiencies and social injustices. This reinforces his earlier critiques of the USSR and China, where he saw bureaucratic control as the primary impediment to genuine socialist development.

V. Yugoslavia and Titoism: Market Socialism Under Scrutiny

Ernest Mandel's analysis of Yugoslavia provided a critical perspective on its unique model, which combined workers' self-management with extensive market mechanisms.

Mandel's Analysis of Yugoslav Workers' Self-Management and Market Mechanisms

Mandel analyzed Yugoslavia as a "unique combination of workers' self-management, extensive use of market mechanisms, and tight political monopoly of power by the Communist League of Yugoslavia". He acknowledged positive aspects, such as "greater workers' initiative and larger span of ideological freedom". The Yugoslav model, driven by Josip Broz Tito, aimed to achieve independence from the Soviet Union following the 1948 Cominform excommunication and economic blockade. This geopolitical context led Yugoslav theorists to critique centralized administrative planning as an inherent source of bureaucracy. The Yugoslav contention was to counter bureaucracy by fostering self-management and self-government, allowing economic units maximum autonomy and use of market mechanisms. This analysis of Yugoslavia highlights the inherent paradox of attempting a "third way" between state socialism and capitalism. While the Yugoslav model aimed to overcome Soviet-style bureaucracy through market mechanisms and self-management, it introduced new contradictions rather than fundamentally resolving them. This suggests that hybrid models, while appearing pragmatic, can introduce new forms of inequality and bureaucratic control. This understanding reinforces his broader thesis that the fundamental contradictions of class society cannot be wished away by institutional design alone; rather, they require a deeper transformation of power relations and the mode of production.

Critiques of Increasing Social Inequality and the Persistence of Bureaucratic Control

Mandel strongly argued that the "increased use of market mechanisms must lead to increased inequality". He cited the actual evolution of Yugoslav society, which showed "growing inequality of income between the different republics, between workers and managers, and inside the working class itself" over a ten-year period. He criticized the Yugoslav premise that centralized planning was the *only* or *main* source of bureaucracy. While it fostered a *central* bureaucracy, Mandel contended that decentralization and market mechanisms did not prevent the growth of *other types and layers of bureaucracy* at the plant and commune levels.

Mandel asserted that if a firm's income depended on profit from competition, it was "impossible to ensure an 'identity of interests of the firm and of the community'". This would inevitably lead to waste, monopolistic behavior, and the production of luxury goods over basic needs due to unequal income distribution. He noted that despite formal workers' councils, the Yugoslav model suffered from an "authoritarian political monopoly" and "bureaucratic and managerial dominance." Workers' councils rarely proposed alternative economic plans, and administrators often held an information advantage, effectively controlling decisions. Mandel highlighted that the Communist Party (renamed the "League of Communists") and state machinery were "not self-liquidating" and retained a "leading position in society," manipulating supposedly "self-governing" structures.

This detailed critique of Yugoslav market socialism reveals a deeper understanding of the intricate relationship between economic mechanisms and social outcomes. The introduction of market forces, even under the guise of workers' self-management, inherently generates inequality and reinforces bureaucratic power at local levels, rather than dissolving it. This implies that market mechanisms, by their very nature, prioritize profit and competition, which are antithetical to socialist goals of equality and collective planning, unless they are strictly subordinated to democratic control at a macro-level. The persistence of a "tight political monopoly" alongside market reforms demonstrates that economic liberalization without genuine political democratization can lead to a *re-entrenchment* of bureaucratic power, albeit in a different form, rather than its dissolution. This suggests that economic "efficiency" gained through marketization often comes at the cost of core socialist principles if not democratically managed and controlled from below.

Comparison with Stalinist Models and the "Shared Weaknesses"

Mandel contended that, despite their differing approaches to economic organization, the "Stalinist and Yugoslav models share the same weaknesses" regarding the problem of bureaucracy. He argued that while over-centralized planning in the USSR fostered a central bureaucracy, the decentralization and market mechanisms in Yugoslavia strengthened bureaucracy at the plant and commune levels, leading to similar issues of waste and inefficiency. This assertion that both Stalinist and Yugoslav models shared "the same weaknesses" concerning bureaucracy is a profound analytical observation. It suggests that bureaucracy is not solely a product of over-centralized, administrative planning (as in Stalinism) but can also manifest and entrench itself within decentralized, market-oriented "socialist" systems (as in Yugoslavia). This implies that the problem of bureaucracy is endemic to *any* post-capitalist state where genuine, comprehensive workers' democracy and direct control over the social surplus product are absent. It shifts the focus from the *form* of economic organization (central planning vs. market mechanisms) to the underlying *power relations* and the degree of popular control, suggesting that the "withering away of the state" is not an automatic outcome of nationalization or marketization but requires a conscious, democratic struggle against privileged layers.

VI. Responding to the "Socialism in One Country" Charge

Ernest Mandel's theoretical framework was fundamentally shaped by his consistent and vigorous opposition to Joseph Stalin's theory of "socialism in one country," which he viewed as a profound deviation from classical Marxism and a betrayal of the internationalist spirit of revolution.

Mandel's Consistent Opposition to Stalin's Theory, Rooted in Trotsky's Permanent Revolution

Mandel consistently opposed Joseph Stalin's theory of "socialism in one country," which advocated for strengthening socialism internally rather than prioritizing global revolution. He affirmed Leon Trotsky's belief that, given the nature of imperialism, the ultimate victory of socialism or capitalism in the Soviet Union could only be determined on an international scale. Mandel argued that establishing a "true classless society of the 'freely associated producers'" was impossible in an isolated Russia. Such a society required a median level of labor productivity superior to that of the most advanced capitalist countries, and it would be in permanent conflict with the world capitalist market. He warned that the "weight of this antagonism" (military and economic pressure from the world capitalist market) would eventually crush the chances for socialism in the USSR if the revolution did not spread to "advanced capitalist nations". Mandel viewed the Left Opposition's struggle against "socialism in one country" and their simultaneous desire to build a socialist economy in the USSR as "two aspects of the same basic strategy," aimed at creating favorable conditions for the inevitable global conflict between socialist and capitalist forces.

Arguments for the International Scale of Socialist Victory and the Dangers of Isolation

Mandel explicitly asserted that "the problems of building socialism will be solved only by world revolution". Without it, he argued, internal "disproportions, distortions, and extreme contradictions cannot be definitively overcome" within an isolated workers' state. He believed that the initial isolation of revolutions in backward countries inherently led to bureaucratic deformation and degeneration. A broader, international revolution would significantly mitigate this risk by providing a more robust and less isolated environment for socialist development. For Mandel, the theory of permanent revolution, in response to isolated socialist victories, proposed a combined strategy: promoting the extension of the world revolution, beginning to build a socialist economy, and developing socialist democracy.

Mandel's unwavering opposition to "socialism in one country" is not merely a theoretical adherence to Trotsky's legacy but a profound analytical observation into the *structural limitations* of isolated revolutionary states. He consistently argued that even if capitalism is overthrown, the new society remains fundamentally vulnerable to the pressures of the world market, military encirclement, and technological gaps. This constant external pressure, combined with internal underdevelopment, creates fertile ground for bureaucratic deformation , as resources are diverted to defense and the population is subjected to sacrifices, leading to a suppression of democracy. This implies that the "socialist" character of such states is always precarious and "deformed," making genuine, full socialist construction impossible without international expansion.

Critiques of Stalinist Economic Policy and its Consequences

Mandel argued that Stalinist economic policy from 1928 onwards was the "antithesis" of the Left Opposition's proposals. He highlighted that Stalin's "full-scale industrialization" was accompanied by a "lowering, not a raising of real wages," a "catastrophic deterioration, not an improvement of labor conditions," and "colossally increased" administrative expenses. This "monstrous deadweight of the bureaucracy" absorbed the majority of what was extracted from worker consumption. Mandel criticized the forced collectivization of agriculture, noting it led to "desperate resistance by the peasants" (including massive slaughter of livestock) and resulted in "misery in the countryside and poverty in the towns for decades". He underscored Trotsky's critique of the bureaucracy's belief that it could create a faultless economic plan without market control and Soviet democracy, leading to systemic "waste" and "low quality" production.

Mandel's detailed critique of Stalinist economic policies transcends a simple moral condemnation. He meticulously demonstrates a causal link between the "socialism in one country" doctrine, the forced "superindustrialization" and collectivization, and the resulting immense human cost (low wages, poor working conditions, widespread peasant misery). This analysis shows that the bureaucratic regime, in its attempt to rapidly industrialize in isolation, systematically suppressed the interests of the workers and peasants, diverting the social surplus not into genuine socialist development but into its own expanding administrative apparatus and coercive state machinery. This is a key understanding of how a non-capitalist state can still generate profound exploitation and waste, not driven by capitalist profit but by bureaucratic self-preservation and the accumulation of power.

VII. Specific Economic Analysis: Distinguishing the USSR from Capitalism

Ernest Mandel's most significant contribution to Marxist political economy was his detailed analysis of the Soviet Union, which he categorized as a unique "transitional society" distinct from both capitalism and genuine socialism.

Mandel's Concept of the Soviet Union as a "Transitional Society" (Neither Capitalist Nor Socialist)

Mandel argued that the Soviet economy constituted a "transitional society" between capitalism and socialism, characterized by "relations of production specific to this transitional period". He maintained that the USSR was no longer capitalist due to state ownership of all major industrial, transportation, and financial enterprises, the legal suppression of private appropriation, centralized economic planning, and a state monopoly of foreign trade. These factors implied the absence of generalized commodity production and the rule of the law of value, meaning there was no market for large means of production or labor-power, and labor-power had ceased to be a commodity. However, he also stressed that it was "not yet socialism" because partial

commodity production (primarily consumer goods) still survived, and the society was characterized by "essentially bourgeois norms of distribution".

Mandel's conceptualization of the USSR as a "transitional society" represents a crucial theoretical innovation within Marxism. This nuanced categorization allowed him to move beyond the simplistic binary of "capitalism or socialism," which often led to analytical dead ends. By defining the Soviet system as neither fully capitalist (lacking generalized commodity production and the driving force of profit) nor fully socialist (lacking genuine workers' democracy and the complete abolition of commodity relations), he provided a framework for understanding its unique internal dynamics, contradictions, and eventual trajectory. This framework was essential for explaining why the Soviet economy behaved differently from both capitalist and genuinely socialist economies, and why its ultimate collapse could not be adequately explained by traditional capitalist crisis theories.

Analysis of Soviet Planning, the Absence of the Profit Motive, and Bureaucratic Privileges

Mandel observed that the absence of the "rule" of the law of value allowed the Soviet economy to develop independently from profit-derived sector priorities and distortions imposed by international capitalism. This enabled it to avoid the business cycle, periodic crises of overproduction, and large-scale unemployment, leading to superior long-term growth rates compared to industrialized capitalist countries, especially during its basic industrialization phase. However, he identified the "un-folding conflict between the logic of the plan and the influence of the law of value" (due to partial commodity pro-duction and world market pressure) as the main contradiction and law of mo-tion of the Soviet economy.

He argued that management by a privileged bureaucracy necessarily in-troduced "enormous distortions and waste in the planning process".

Bureaucratic privileges, according to Mandel, were primarily restricted to consumption—manifesting as higher money incomes (often illegally ac-quired) and non-monetary advantages like access to special shops, cars, and housing. Crucially, these privileges did *not* lead to private ownership of the means of production or the accumula-tion of vast private fortunes.

Mandel argued that this was a key theoretical proof that the bureaucracy was *not* a new ruling class, because a genuine ruling class's basic material in-terests would align with the logic of the mode of production it represented (e.g., capitalists' interests align with capital accumulation). The Soviet bu-reaucracy's material self-interest (in consumption) fundamentally clashed with the optimal functioning of a planned economy, leading to systemic waste (e.g., hiding reserves, false infor-mation, low-quality outputs, under-em-ployment of capacity).

This observation highlights that the bureaucracy's consumption-driven interests conflict with the optimal func-tioning of a planned economy, leading to systemic waste and proving it is not a new ruling class.

Arguments Against "State Capitalism"

Mandel systematically demolished the "state capitalism" theory, particu-larly in response to critics like Michael Kidron. He argued that Kidron's defi-nitions of capitalism were flawed be-cause they could apply to other class societies. For Mandel, the specific char-acteristic of capitalism is the **generali-zation of commodity production**, where all elements of production, in-cluding labor power, become commod-ities, leading to universal competition and the relentless drive for capital accu-mulation. He differentiated this from pre-capitalist societies, where growth was primarily in use-values, and disor-ders stemmed from underproduction, contrasting with capitalism's crises of overproduction of exchange-values.

Mandel refuted the idea that "leaks" like wars or capital exports in-sulated capitalism from its inherent contradictions. He argued that slumps are the destruction of *capital as value*, which is an internal "safety-valve" in Marx's model, not an external leak. Capital exports are a manifestation of capitalism's basic law of motion, flow-ing to higher profit rates, and war pro-duction contributes to accumulation like any other industry.

Regarding the Soviet economy, Mandel asserted that if there was a "sin-gle capital" and no competition, then there was a "central, public arrange-ment" (central planning), which is un-attainable under capitalism. He used the analogy of General Motors: within GM, there's no capitalist competition between departments; goods flow as use-values. GM is capitalist because its *final products are commodities sold on a market* in competition with other firms. If a collectivized entity does not sell commodities on an outside market, it would not be capitalist. There would be no capital accumulation (only accumulation of industrial equipment as use-values), no flow of capital based on profitability, and no cyclical crises or unemployment. While external threats from capitalism influenced the Soviet economy, these were *external pressures*, not the *internal laws of motion* of capitalism.

Mandel's rejection of "state capitalism" and his defense of the transitional society concept was crucial for maintaining a revolutionary perspective and understanding the unique contradictions of post-capitalist states. He argued that the "state capitalism" theory led to a "useless and dangerous revolutionary strategy" by implying that world capitalism was stronger than ever, thus discouraging socialist revolution.

He also pointed out the inconsistency of "state capitalists" who refused to back North Korea and China against American imperialism but then supported North Vietnam, revealing the theoretical flaws. He denied that capitalism could be restored "gradually" in the Soviet Union, believing the working class would fiercely resist such a disintegration.

VIII. Position on Democratic Rights Under Socialism

Mandel's vision of socialism was inextricably linked with the broadest possible democratic rights, viewing them not as a bourgeois luxury but as an indispensable component for the successful construction of a classless society.

Advocacy for Unlimited Political Democracy, Multi-Party Systems, and Press Freedom

Mandel consistently advocated for unlimited political democracy under socialism, including multi-party and multi-platform democracy, which he believed could not be implemented without unlimited freedom of the press. He proposed a system where every civilian group would be guaranteed access to printing presses and media, strictly proportional to the support they could mobilize, verified by signatures, sales, or viewing audience. For instance, 20,000 people might secure the right to publish a daily paper, while smaller groups could publish weeklies or monthlies.

The only constraint on this freedom, in his view, was material: a nationwide body would allocate a percentage of total resources to the media, and media sector producers could not be forced to exceed a democratically decided workload.

Mandel explicitly stated that this material limitation did not restrict the freedom of individuals to express their ideas. He argued that any restriction based on "objectivity," "fairness," or "responsibility" potentially undermines press freedom for all, as criteria for "objectivity" are subjective and can change, leading to censorship.

He aligned with Marx's polemics against censorship, viewing "irresponsible," "subjective" reporting, and "disinformation" as lesser evils than censorship.

Truth Through Debate and Self-Education

Mandel believed that limiting press freedom hinders the building of socialism because there are no final "rules" or "laws" about socialism. Society during this period is a "huge laboratory of successive, often contradictory experiments," and mistakes are inevitable.

The key is to limit and quickly correct mistakes, which requires the fullest expression of minority counterproposals while majority proposals are being developed. This, in turn, necessitates unlimited political democracy and press freedom. He rejected the idea of infallibility (e.g., "The party is always right"), arguing that truth is never final and can only be discovered through the fullest possible debate and freedom of opinion. He cited Friedrich Engels, who stated that the Party needs socialist science, which cannot develop without the fullest freedom of movement. Mandel emphasized that freedom of the press is inseparable from the flourishing of socialist democracy and multi-party/multi-platform democracy, referencing Rosa Luxemburg's prophecy that restricting political freedoms to a single-party system would lead to the disappearance of political life from the Soviets, leaving only bureaucracy as an active factor.

Mandel's unwavering commitment to unlimited political democracy is a defining feature of his vision for socialism. His arguments that censorship and single-party rule are detrimental, even counter-productive, to socialist construction highlight a fundamental belief that genuine social progress and the "discovery of truth" require open debate and the "right of error for majorities". This position directly contrasts with the bureaucratic regimes he critiqued, where political control stifled economic rationality and human development. This implies that socialist transformation is not merely about nationalizing means of production but about empowering the working masses to collectively and democratically shape their own destiny, making democracy not a luxury but an essential functional requirement for building a qualitatively better society.

Economic Freedom and Producers'/Consumers' Democracy

Mandel asserted that the need to extend human rights and freedom to the economic sphere does not conflict with unlimited press freedom.

Economic freedom for producers to control their lives and working conditions depends on suppressing private ownership of large means of production and exchange, and emancipation from market laws, profit motives, and capital accumulation. It also hinges on their right and power to escape "either state despotism or market despotism" and to freely, collectively, and consciously decide what to produce, how to produce, and how to distribute a significant part of the output.

Since producer/consumers are not homogeneous in their interests or understanding, differences of opinion about priorities are unavoidable. If multi-party, multi-platform democracy and press freedom are restricted, sectors of the working class will be restricted in their economic freedom.

Economic freedom at macro-economic and macro-social levels requires the possibility for toilers to choose among alternative proposals for economic development and coherent development plans, which cannot be realized without the fullest freedom of discussion and press.

IX. Response to Sectarian Criticisms Within Trotskyism

Ernest Mandel's leadership within the Fourth International was marked by his active engagement in internal debates and his consistent efforts to combat sectarianism, which he viewed as detrimental to the revolutionary movement.

Internal Debates and Splits (Pablo, Cannon, Healy)

Mandel was deeply involved in the internal struggles of the Fourth International, particularly the contentious Pablo-Cannon split in the early 1950s, which led to a ten year division in the FI Initially, Mandel was broadly aligned with Michel Pablo, supporting his theses on "entryism in the mass workers' parties, Communist or Socialist according to the country," in anticipation of a "coming war". This support, though with some critical distance (reflected in Mandel's Ten Theses on Stalinism), led to accusations of sacrificing his own opinions for unity with Pablo, particularly when entry into the French Communist Party was imposed authoritatively, causing a split.

However, Mandel played a crucial role in the partial reunification of the International in 1963, following a friendly meeting with James P. Cannon, the leader of the US Socialist Workers Party (SWP). At the 1963 reunification Congress, Mandel presented his thesis on the "three sectors of the world revolution" (proletarian revolution in advanced capitalist countries, colonial revolution, and political revolution in the countries of the East), which marked a significant theoretical departure from Pablo's more "Third Worldist" leanings.

This engagement with sectarian criticisms illustrates the challenges of maintaining theoretical and organizational unity within a revolutionary movement. His consistent polemic against "myopia of sectarians" and his efforts to reunite the Fourth International demonstrate a commitment to a broad, principled revolutionary front, even when faced with significant theoretical disagreements. This approach emphasizes the dialectical relationship between theoretical clarity and political effectiveness in a fragmented revolutionary landscape.

Mandel also fiercely polemicized against Gerry Healy, a prominent figure in British Trotskyism, whom he accused of reducing the class struggle to "police infiltration and operations of agents". Mandel dismissed Healy's slanders as "stupid" and a "Stalinist depth" that deformed Marxism, arguing that such accusations gave "aid and comfort to all the slanders and all the attacks which for such a long period have been conducted against our movement" by both Stalinism and imperialism. He expressed pity for Healy, attributing his degeneration to the "accumulation of the logic of sectarian mistakes".

Mandel's Stance Against "Ultra-Leftism" and "Myopia of Sectarians"

Mandel consistently positioned himself against what he termed the "myopia of sectarians" and "ultra-leftism". He believed that such tendencies hindered the practical task of building a mass revolutionary party. His last major polemical work, "Sectarian vs. Revolutionary Marxism" (in the *Bulletin in Defense of Marxism*, May 1995), reiterated his basic contention that the Fourth International's path to becoming a mass international would likely involve "regroupments and fusions," provided they occurred on the basis of a correct program and fully respected internal democracy, the right of tendency, and the non-prohibition of factions. He argued that such mergers and fusions were a guiding principle, based on the history of the Russian Revolution and the Bolshevik party prior to Stalinism.

Defense of the Fourth International and Principled Activity

Mandel tirelessly defended the Fourth International against attacks, emphasizing its growing strength and rootedness in the working class. He cited examples of the International's practical solidarity and effectiveness, such as immediate trade union support in Peru for a tortured comrade, successful intervention to secure Tariq Ali's release in Pakistan, and factory strikes in Spain that led to the release of 154 arrested Basque comrades. These examples, he argued, proved that the Fourth International was a "genuine part of the international working class movement" and that slandering it would yield "zero point zero" results.

He attributed the Fourth International's resilience to its adherence to a "very simple, a very consistent, and a very, very, very difficult way," which involved "sticking to confidence in the working class; confidence in the class struggle; participating in the class struggle, participating in mass action, educating our members and educating the working class in relentless and irreconcilable struggle against every form of exploitation and oppression in the world". He stressed the importance of a "correct program," telling the truth to workers, and not resorting to "slanders" or "false accusations". Mandel argued that by adhering to this principled line, they had successfully resisted "terrible odds," including the slanders and murders committed by Stalin and Hitler, and had transmitted their heritage to a new, stronger generation.

X. Analysis of Post-War Revolutionary Movements

Mandel's analysis of post-war revolutionary movements was characterized by a global perspective, encapsulated in his framework of the "three sectors of the world revolution."

Global Context and the "Three Sectors of the World Revolution"

Mandel articulated a comprehensive framework for understanding global revolutionary processes, identifying three interconnected "sectors of the world revolution": the proletarian revolution in advanced capitalist countries, the colonial revolution in underdeveloped countries, and the political (anti-bureaucratic) revolution in the bureaucratized workers' states (like the

USSR and China). This framework allowed for a nuanced understanding of how global capitalism creates diverse points of rupture and how struggles in one region influence others. He emphasized that the victory of the world revolution still remained ahead, but the historical period beginning with the fall of Mussolini in 1943 and the transformation of the Yugoslav resistance movement into a proletarian revolution marked the progression of the world revolution, with the Chinese revolution in 1949 being a major factor.

Mandel's "three sectors of the world revolution" framework is a sophisticated analytical tool that goes beyond a linear or singular view of revolutionary change. By identifying distinct but interconnected arenas of struggle, he emphasized that global capitalism creates diverse points of rupture. This perspective avoids "Third Worldism" by stressing that while colonial revolutions weaken imperialism, they cannot overthrow it definitively without the working class in advanced capitalist countries playing its decisive role.

Similarly, anti-bureaucratic revolutions in the East strengthen the global working class. This understanding underscores that the world revolution is a complex, multi-faceted process, where advances in one sector can influence and accelerate struggles in others, demonstrating a truly global and dialectical approach to revolutionary strategy.

Support for National Liberation Movements (Vietnam, Cuba)

Mandel was a staunch supporter of national liberation movements, viewing them as integral to the global revolutionary process. He recognized that national liberation movements in colonial and semi-colonial countries, with their potential to develop into socialist revolutions under adequate proletarian leadership, were "part and parcel of the process of world revolution".

He expressed strong solidarity with the Cuban Revolution, praising its social achievements and its role as an "advanced bastion of the emancipation of man". He also vehemently condemned American imperialism's actions in Vietnam, calling for a "global revolutionary strategy" to counter the global counter-revolutionary strategy of imperialism. He criticized the majority of Communist parties for advocating "peace" and "negotiations" instead of mobilizing masses for the National Liberation Front's victory, and for their failure to organize protest strikes against the war. He believed that American imperialism was calculating risks and increasing escalation because it was convinced neither the USSR nor China would intervene directly. He called for the Soviet government to publicly declare that any attack on China would be considered an attack on the Soviet Union.

Critique of "Third Worldism" and Emphasis on the Working Class in Imperialist Countries

While supporting liberation movements, Mandel critically engaged with "Third Worldism," which he saw as fallacious for writing off the American working class from any medium-term revolutionary perspective. He argued that revolutionary Marxists do not believe that the loss of colonial domains automatically creates a revolutionary situation in imperialist countries; rather, these losses have revolutionary effects only if they trigger internal material changes. He emphasized the "necessary mediation" of changes in the economy, class relations, and consciousness within imperialist society.

Mandel maintained that while imperialism exploits workers and peasants globally, it also maintains and strengthens differences between societies. He argued that the "decisive battle for world socialism can only be fought by the German, British, Japanese, French, Italian and American workers". This perspective underscored the universal law of uneven and combined development, explaining why the first victorious socialist revolutions occurred in underdeveloped countries (Russia, Yugoslavia, China) but also why the ultimate overthrow of imperialism required the proletariat in advanced capitalist nations.

Analysis of Anti-Bureaucratic Revolutions (Hungary, Czechoslovakia)

Mandel incorporated the lessons from the explosive events of Hungary in 1956 and Czechoslovakia in 1968-69 into his analysis of anti-bureaucratic revolutions, viewing them as historical confirmations of the inevitability of political revolution against the bureaucracy. He argued that these events demonstrated "the ease and rapidity with which the masses were able to dominate the bureaucracy, precisely because the latter is not *a class*". He noted that in each instance, "the intervention of an external military force was necessary to prevent a rapid triumph of the developing political revolution, almost without serious cost in human terms". This observation reinforced his argument that the bureaucracy, unlike a capitalist class, lacks the inherent social power to withstand mass mobilization without external military intervention.

He acknowledged that bureaucratic regimes could implement reforms, sometimes "very bold ones," as a price for survival, citing the concessions in Hungary in 1956 and the reforms in Czechoslovakia in 1968. However, he asserted that "these reforms come up against an insurmountable barrier of social interests when they endanger the material privileges of the bureaucracy," such as any real sovereignty of workers' councils or restoration of unrestricted democratic rights. Thus, reforms would halt before challenging the Communist Party's monopoly of power, only transforming into genuine revolution from below through powerful mass mobilizations.

XI. Theoretical Methodology and Dialectical Approach

Ernest Mandel's intellectual rigor was deeply rooted in his consistent application and creative development of the Marxist dialectical method, which he saw as essential for understanding the dynamic and contradictory nature of social reality.

Emphasis on Dialectical Materialism

Mandel's entire theoretical edifice rested upon dialectical materialism, which he understood as a method for analyzing social phenomena in their "inner connection as an integrated totality, structured around, and by, a basic predominant mode of production". He emphasized that this method starts with a class-determined analysis of phenomena as the "unity in contradiction of relations and process".

This approach allowed him to analyze social reality as dynamic, characterized by the interplay of opposing forces, and constantly evolving. He articulated that phenomena are always both realized and potential, with potential features being opposite and contradictory to their realized aspects, making the unity of identity and difference comprehensible.

Mandel's consistent application of dialectical materialism is not a mere philosophical adherence but a practical methodological commitment. His emphasis on "unity in contradiction" and the dynamic interplay of opposing forces (e.g., between productive forces and relations of production, or between plan and market) allows for a non-deterministic, yet structured, understanding of social change. This approach enabled him to analyze complex phenomena like "late capitalism" and the "deformed workers' states" not as static categories but as evolving systems driven by internal tensions. His rejection of dogmatism and his advocacy for "open Marxism" further underscore his belief that Marxist theory must remain dynamic and responsive to new historical developments, constantly refining its categories through empirical study and critical debate. This methodological flexibility was crucial for his ability to analyze the complexities of the 20th century without resorting to rigid schemas.

Unity of Theory and Practice

For Mandel, Marxism was not merely an academic pursuit but a "guide to action". He vigorously argued for the "indispensable integration of theory and practice". He believed that conscious action for emancipation could not be carried on effectively unless one understood the social environment, the forces to confront, and the general social and economic conditions of the liberation movement. This meant understanding the motive forces behind social and economic evolution to transform it into revolution. He viewed science as serving the proletarian cause only insofar as it gathered genuine knowledge and helped draw the right political conclusions.

Analysis of Contradictions

Mandel applied the classical Marxist laws of dialectics: the unity and conflict of opposites, the passage of quantitative into qualitative changes, and the negation of the negation. He saw contradictions as inherent in social relations, leading to mutual development. For instance, in capitalism, the social surplus takes the monetary form of surplus value, driving accumulation and technological development, yet this system based on private ownership and profit maximization also leads to immense waste, crises of overproduction, and social constraints on needs. This demonstrates the unity of opposites within the capitalist system itself. He also highlighted how the productive forces released by capitalism could turn into destructive forces if capitalism is not destroyed, a prediction he saw fulfilled in the era of the atomic bomb and ecological crises.

Rejection of Dogmatism and "Open Marxism"

Mandel was a vocal critic of dogmatism within Marxism. He engaged in debates, notably with Johannes Agnoli, which led to their co-authored book *Offener Marxismus: Ein Gespräch über Dogmen, Orthodoxie und die Häresie der Realität* (Open Marxism: A Discussion about Doctrines, Orthodoxy and the Heresy of Reality). This concept of "open Marxism" emphasized a critique of state socialism and party politics, stressing the need for openness to praxis and history through an anti-positivist method grounded in Marx's own concepts. It advocated for a non-deterministic view of history, foregrounding the unpredictability of class struggle. Mandel also argued against the idea of an "epistemological break" in Marx's thought, asserting instead an "important evolution, not identical repetition, in Marx's thought from decade to decade". He criticized approaches that veered too much from Marxist orthodoxy, which he treated as a doctrine that needed to be creatively developed, not rigidly adhered to.

XII. Conclusions

Ernest Mandel's intellectual legacy is defined by his profound commitment to a dynamic, undogmatic Marxism, meticulously applied to the complex realities of the 20th century. His analyses consistently sought to discern the underlying laws of motion in both capitalist and post-capitalist societies, while simultaneously emphasizing the crucial role of conscious human agency in historical transformation.

His unwavering opposition to "socialism in one country" was a cornerstone of his thought, rooted in the understanding that genuine socialist construction could not be achieved in isolation but required the international extension of revolution. He demonstrated how the pressures of the world market and military encirclement inevitably led to bureaucratic deformation and economic distortions in isolated post-capitalist states, whether in the Stalinist USSR or Titoist Yugoslavia. His detailed economic analysis of the Soviet Union as a "transitional society" —neither capitalist nor fully socialist— provided a unique framework for understanding its internal contradictions, distinguishing it from capitalism by the absence of generalized commodity production and the profit motive, yet highlighting its systemic waste due to bureaucratic self-interest.

Mandel's critical embrace of the Cuban Revolution, particularly his alignment with Che Guevara on the necessity of consciously "violating" the law of value for underdeveloped nations to industrialize, underscored his belief that socialist planning must prioritize long-term social development over immediate market profitability. Across all these analyses, a central theme was the indispensable role of robust workers' democracy. He argued that genuine socialist transformation, free from bureaucratic degeneration, required unlimited political democracy, multi-party systems, and full freedom of the press, viewing these as functional necessities for rational economic planning and the self-emancipation of the working class.

His engagement with sectarian criticisms within the Trotskyist movement further illuminated his commitment to principled revolutionary unity and his rejection of dogmatism. He consistently argued against "ultra-leftism" and the "myopia of sectarians," advocating for broad regroupments and fusions based on programmatic agreement and internal democracy. Finally, his framework of the "three sectors of the world revolution" provided a sophisticated understanding of the interconnected nature of global revolutionary processes, recognizing diverse points of struggle while emphasizing the decisive role of the working class in advanced capitalist countries for the ultimate overthrow of imperialism.

In sum, Mandel's work offers a powerful testament to the vitality of Marxist theory when applied with intellectual rigor, empirical responsiveness, and an unwavering commitment to democratic principles. His analytical framework continues to provide valuable tools for understanding the complexities of global capitalism, the challenges of post-capitalist transitions, and the enduring necessity of a democratic, international socialist project.

Ernest Mandel: Some of his Contributions to Marxist Theory and Revolutionary Practice

I. Personal Exchanges and Their Political Significance

Ernest Mandel's intellectual and political trajectory was not merely an academic pursuit; it was profoundly shaped by his direct interactions and leadership roles within the international revolutionary movement. These engagements frequently served as crucial arenas for the development of his theoretical positions and the formulation of practical strategies.

I.1. Interactions with Che Guevara and Shared Economic Views

Ernest Mandel's intellectual influence extended directly into the heart of revolutionary governments, exemplified by his invitation to Cuba in the spring of 1964 by Che Guevara, then Minister of Industry. Guevara held Mandel's Marxist Economic Theory in high regard, leading to an extensive seven-week visit during which Mandel engaged in numerous discussions with Che and other Cuban leaders.

Their exchanges revealed a significant alignment on fundamental economic principles. Both Mandel and Guevara maintained that products exchanged between nationalized enterprises were not commodities, and therefore, the law of value should not govern production within the state or public sector. They advocated for the financing of enterprises primarily through the State budget, aligning with a centralized planning model, and explicitly opposed self-financing systems. A core tenet of their shared economic outlook was the conviction that industrialization in underdeveloped nations

necessitated a deliberate "violation of the law of value." This approach prioritized long-term economic and social development over immediate profitability, as they believed that reliance on market mechanisms would inevitably perpetuate underdevelopment. Mandel also cautioned against the perils of excessive autonomy for enterprises in underdeveloped contexts, arguing that such autonomy could lead to local or sectoral interests superseding national development objectives, thereby impeding overall industrialization.

During these substantive discussions, Mandel actively sought to impress upon Guevara the critical importance of establishing a robust socialist democracy. He emphasized that genuine workers' management at the enterprise level and comprehensive workers' democracy at the state level, including the formation of a national congress of workers' committees, were indispensable safeguards against bureaucratic deformation. This direct engagement with Che Guevara in Cuba represents a compelling instance where abstract Marxist economic theory was brought into immediate dialogue with the practical challenges of constructing socialism in a post-revolutionary, underdeveloped nation. The shared understanding between Mandel and Che regarding central planning and the conscious "violation of the law of value" underscored a mutual conviction that revolutionary economic transformation required a deliberate departure from capitalist logic. This interaction highlights Mandel's role as a militant scholar, demonstrating that his Marxism was not merely an academic exercise but a dynamic framework designed to inform and guide real-world revolutionary processes. It underscored the practical application and intellectual influence of his work within the global revolutionary movement.

Mandel maintained close ties with Cuba after his visits and penned a poignant tribute to Che Guevara following his assassination in October 1967, mourning him as a "dear comrade".

I.2. Role in the Fourth International's Internal Debates and Reunification Efforts

Ernest Mandel's revolutionary convictions were deeply ingrained, stemming from a family background steeped in anti-Stalinist radicalism, and his own active role in building Trotskyism concurrently with the Resistance during World War II. His involvement in the internal dynamics of the Fourth International (FI) was both central and at times contentious.

Mandel played a significant, albeit controversial, role in the 1953 split within the FI. He aligned with Michel Pablo, supporting the "entryism" tactic—where Trotskyists would join larger, established mass workers' parties—and the theoretical concept of "centuries of deformed workers' states". This stance drew considerable criticism from orthodox Trotskyists, notably James P. Cannon, who viewed these positions as fundamental revisions of Trotskyist principles. Critics also pointed to Mandel's defense of Pablo's bureaucratic methods and his belief that the Stalinist bureaucracy could undergo a process of "self-reform" under mass pressure, potentially

leading to a "real liquidation of the Stalinist regime" through internal bureaucratic struggles rather than a mass political revolution.

Despite these profound ideological and organizational divisions, a partial reunification of the Fourth International was achieved in 1963, notably after a "friendly meeting" between Mandel and James P. Cannon. This reunification saw Mandel co-authoring a programmatic statement that established common ground on the dynamics of world revolution. A significant theoretical contribution by Mandel at the 1963 reunification congress was his thesis on the "three sectors of the world revolution": the proletarian revolution in advanced capitalist countries, the colonial revolution, and the political revolution in the bureaucratized "workers' states" of the East. This framework represented a crucial theoretical advancement and a departure from Pablo's more exclusive focus on "Third Worldism". Following Pablo's departure from the now-renamed United Secretariat of the Fourth International (USec/ USFI) in 1965, Mandel became the organization's principal spokesman.

In 1977, Mandel vehemently denounced Gerry Healy's "frame-up campaign" against the Fourth International, accusing Healy of reducing the complexities of class struggle to mere "police infiltration and operations of agents". Mandel passionately defended the FI's integrity and its deep connections within the international working class, asserting that such slanders would ultimately "boomerang against himself". Mandel's complex involvement in the internal struggles of the Fourth International, particularly the 1953 split and the 1963 reunification, demonstrates his strategic flexibility and persistent commitment to international revolutionary organization amidst profound ideological differences. His initial support for Pablo's controversial theories and his later participation in the reunification with Cannon's faction, along with his presentation of the "three sectors" thesis, illustrate an evolution in his strategic thinking, perhaps reflecting a recognition of the limitations of earlier positions or the imperative of broader unity. His willingness to engage with former adversaries and his subsequent role as a leading spokesman for the reunified FI underscore a pragmatic commitment to consolidating the international movement. His forceful condemnation of Healy's sectarianism further highlights his dedication to protecting the organizational integrity and public standing of the Fourth International, viewing such attacks as detrimental to the broader class struggle. For Mandel, theoretical clarity and organizational unity were inextricably linked to effective revolutionary practice.

I.3. Engagement with Student Movements and Activists

Beginning in 1968, Ernest Mandel gained widespread public recognition as a prominent Marxist politician. He embarked on extensive speaking tours across student campuses in Europe and America, delivering lectures on a range of topics including socialism, imperialism, and revolution.

He actively engaged with influential student leaders of the era, such as Rudi Dutschke and Alain Krivine, during the summers and winters of 1967. Their discussions centered on critical strategic questions and the vital task of establishing a vanguard organization within the Students for a Democratic Society (SDS). Mandel held "highest expectations" for the burgeoning movements in Germany and played a central role as a key speaker at the Vietnam congress held in Berlin in February 1968. At this event, he advocated for decisive actions by a revolutionary vanguard comprising young individuals, estimated at 15,000 to 20,000 students and young workers.

Mandel's analytical approach to student movements extended beyond viewing them as isolated revolts against immediate academic conditions. He interpreted them as manifestations of deeper societal contradictions, particularly in underdeveloped countries where various forces impelled youth to rise up. Mandel's direct and sustained engagement with student movements, especially during the politically charged late 1960s, underscores his strategic understanding of the pivotal role of youth in revolutionary processes. His discussions on "vanguard organization" and "effective actions" demonstrated his commitment to translating theoretical insights into practical organizational forms for a new generation of activists. By interpreting student revolts as symptoms of broader "social contradictions," Mandel provided a Marxist framework for comprehending these movements, aiming to integrate them into a larger revolutionary strategy. This active participation highlights

Mandel's belief in the necessity of a conscious, organized "subjective factor"—a revolutionary party or cadre—to guide spontaneous mass discontent towards socialist transformation, thereby preventing its dissipation or cooptation.

II. Detailed Analysis of Specific Countries and Revolutionary Movements

Ernest Mandel consistently applied his theoretical framework to concrete historical developments, offering nuanced and often critical analyses of various "socialist" experiments and liberation movements across the globe. His analytical focus consistently centered on discerning the underlying class dynamics and the extent to which these societies genuinely progressed towards, or deviated from, a classless, democratic socialist future.

II.1. Yugoslavia: Critique of Self-Management, Market Mechanisms, and Bureaucratic Control

Ernest Mandel characterized the Yugoslav Workers' Self-Management (YWSM) as a "unique combination" of workers' self-management, extensive market mechanisms, and the Communist League of Yugoslavia's tight political monopoly of power. While acknowledging positive aspects such as "greater workers' initiative" and a "larger span of ideological freedom," he heavily emphasized the negative consequences, including "increasing social inequality" and an "increasing abdication of central planning".

Mandel criticized the "vague theory of self-management" in Yugoslavia,

asserting that the model shared fundamental weaknesses with Stalinist systems, particularly concerning the inherent contradictions introduced by market mechanisms. He specifically critiqued Branko Horvat's theoretical justifications for the Yugoslav model, arguing that Horvat's approach was more aligned with the Cambridge school of welfare economics than with Marxism. Mandel found Horvat's definition of bureaucracy "ludicrous," equating it merely with "habits of those accustomed to lead from behind an office desk". From a traditional Marxist perspective, Mandel posited a fundamental incompatibility between socialism—defined as a classless society with high social equality and economic efficiency—and commodity production. He argued that commodity production inevitably generates social inequality and reproduces primitive capital accumulation. He contended that the Yugoslav Communists were the first to attempt to reverse this classical Marxist antithesis by intending the market economy to persist even after the construction of socialism, viewing this as a pragmatic and apologetic justification of their country's reality rather than a theoretically sound development.

Mandel defined bureaucracy from a Marxist perspective as "the sum total of all materially privileged elements and layers which are not private owners of the means of production." He argued that decentralization and market mechanisms, far from eliminating bureaucracy, led to its growth at the plant and commune level, alongside increased inequality between different economic units, industrial branches, regions, and between workers and managerial personnel. Mandel's critique of Yugoslavia extends beyond a superficial assessment of its "self-management" claims, delving into the systemic contradictions arising from its unique economic model. He challenged the fundamental Yugoslav premise that a market economy could persist into socialism without reproducing capitalist contradictions, asserting that commodity production inherently generates inequality and waste. He demonstrated that the increased use of market mechanisms, coupled with a lack of genuine democratic control from below, led to increased social inequality and the growth of bureaucracy at decentralized levels, rather than its elimination. This analysis indicated that merely decentralizing economic decision-making without fundamentally altering power relations could lead to new forms of exploitation and privilege. This highlights Mandel's consistent argument that true socialist transformation requires not just nationalization or formal self-management, but a conscious, democratically planned economy that subordinates market logic to social priorities, backed by genuine workers' power. His proposed "democratic centralization" was a direct response to the observed failures, emphasizing that planning is not inherently bureaucratic but becomes so in the absence of democratic accountability.

As an alternative, Mandel proposed a model of "democratic centralization" for Yugoslavia. This model would achieve demand and supply equalization a priori through a central plan, with market mechanisms used only to adjust consumer goods prices

within these centrally determined limits. He envisioned a federal central body of workers' councils with supreme authority, operating under strict conditions to prevent bureaucratization, thereby strengthening and unifying the working class.

II.2. China: Critiques of Agricultural Policies, Cultural Revolution, Bureaucratic Methods, and Sino-Soviet Split

Ernest Mandel regarded the "Cultural Revolution" as "the most complex phenomenon faced by revolutionary Marxists in recent decades," emphasizing the need for painstaking analysis rather than simplistic interpretations. He interpreted its "objective meaning" as Mao's deliberate appeal to the masses, bypassing party and state cadres, when facing internal opposition.

Mandel critiqued Mao's agricultural policies, arguing that an overestimation of the peasantry's capacity for sacrifice resulted in "serious setbacks" between 1959-61 and fostered "substantial social differentiation" in Chinese villages, evident in income disparities across "working teams" and regions. He observed that the Red Guard movement, initially focused on student youth, rapidly "escaped control" and prompted broader critiques of the bureaucracy. This compelled the Maoist faction to extend mobilization to industrial plants, giving rise to the "revolutionary rebels" movement. Ultimately, Mandel viewed the Cultural Revolution as a "conflict within the bureaucracy where contending factions appealed to the masses." Its aim, he contended, was a partial change in leadership and political orientation, an attempt to reform the bureaucracy, not to abolish it.

Mandel criticized the systematic organization of the "Mao cult" as serving inter-bureaucratic power struggles rather than genuine democracy, contrasting it with Stalin's ascent, which was facilitated by mass political passivity. He noted the general absence of genuine workers' councils or soviet-type organs in Chinese industrial plants. He further argued that Mao abandoned Marxist sociology by attributing the danger of degeneration to ideological factors rather than the material infrastructure of society, leading to "enormities" such as defining a capitalist based on disagreement with "Mao Tse-tung's thought". Mandel considered the Chinese revolution "deformed" from its inception, with the proletariat playing only a contributory role and a peasant army substituting for independent mass action, resulting in a state and party that were more bureaucratized from the outset than the USSR in 1927.

He primarily attributed the Sino-Soviet split to the Soviet bureaucracy's refusal to provide nuclear weapons or economic aid to China, which severely complicated China's economic and social development. While acknowledging Maoist leaders' "ultra-opportunistic policies" in Indonesia and sectarianism regarding a united front in defense of Vietnam, he emphasized the Soviet bureaucracy's primary responsibility for the Chinese crisis. In his later analyses (1982), Mandel examined China's persistent economic crisis, noting declin-

ing economic growth, rampant inflation, recurring budget deficits, and the relaxation of the "right to work" rule, which resulted in significant urban unemployment and worker protests. He also observed a substantial expansion of the private sector and escalating political repression. Mandel's analysis of the Cultural Revolution as an intra-bureaucratic conflict, rather than a genuine political revolution, provided a critical lens for understanding the dynamics of post-capitalist states. He observed that while the Cultural Revolution, initiated by Mao, aimed to mobilize masses against party cadres, the mass movement, once unleashed, exceeded Mao's initial intentions and began to question the entire bureaucracy, leading to repression and military intervention. The absence of genuine workers' councils and the ideological distortions, such as the subjective definition of "capitalist," allowed the bureaucracy to maintain control, even as its monolithic unity was shattered. This demonstrated that even when a bureaucracy is weakened, it can reassert control if independent, self-organized workers' power is not firmly established. This highlights Mandel's consistent argument that revolutionary change cannot be successfully imposed from above, even by a "revolutionary" leader. Genuine socialist transformation requires the active, self-organized participation of the masses and the institutionalization of their power, which a bureaucracy, by its very nature, will resist. The later economic crises and repression further illustrated the long-term instability caused by unresolved bureaucratic contradictions.

II.3. Cuba: Nuanced Views on the Revolution, Economic Policies, and Bureaucratic Deformation

Ernest Mandel expressed profound admiration for the Cuban Revolution, describing it as "the most advanced bastion of the emancipation of man." He lauded its transformative societal impact, including the conversion of military barracks into schools, the redistribution of luxurious mansions to scholarship students, extensive mass literacy campaigns, the radical suppression of racial inequality, and the elimination of unemployment.

Mandel strongly supported Che Guevara's economic policies, particularly the Budgetary Finance System (BFS), which advocated for financing enterprises through the State budget and aligned with central planning, in contrast to self-financing models. He critiqued Stalin's stance on the law of value, arguing that while the law of value might objectively operate in a socialist economy, it "should not directly regulate production," especially in underdeveloped countries striving for industrialization. He differentiated between violating and merely disregarding the law of value, emphasizing the necessity of strict cost calculation while consciously prioritizing long-term social development over immediate profitability. Mandel consistently warned against the adoption of pro-market reforms, believing they would lead to social injustices, speculation, and a distortion of the central plan, thereby recreating an economic logic more akin to capitalism.

Mandel contended that the primary threat of bureaucracy did not reside in centralization itself, but rather in the "absence of workers' democracy at the national political level." Citing Trotsky, he stressed that "only the coordination of three elements, state planning, the market and Soviet democracy, can assure correct guidance of the economy of the epoch of transition". He advocated for genuine workers' management at the enterprise level and robust workers' democracy at the state level as essential safeguards against bureaucratization. He believed that democratically established priorities for centralized investments, guided by a national congress of workers' councils, would effectively suppress sources of bureaucracy. Mandel's analysis of Cuba revealed a critical balance between celebrating revolutionary achievements and identifying potential pitfalls, particularly concerning economic management and democratic control. His high praise for Cuba's social and economic transformations, viewing them as a beacon of human emancipation, was coupled with his support for Che Guevara's economic model, which consciously sought to "violate the law of value." This demonstrated his conviction that overcoming underdevelopment required a deliberate, planned approach that transcended capitalist profit logic, rather than simply replicating market mechanisms. Mandel's warnings against market reforms and excessive enterprise autonomy illustrated his understanding that without democratic control, these elements could lead to new forms of inequality and bureaucratic power, thereby undermining the very goals of the revolution. This underscored Mandel's core argument that nationalization of the means of production is a necessary, but not sufficient, condition for socialism. The success of a post-capitalist society, especially in overcoming underdevelopment, critically hinges on the democratic nature of planning and the active participation of the working class at all levels, from the enterprise to the national state. This was his proposed defense against the "logic that was to lead to a faithful, if not servile, imitation of Stalinist theory".

II.4. Poland: Analysis of the Economic Crisis and the Role of Solidarity

Ernest Mandel meticulously analyzed the severe economic crisis that afflicted Poland from 1979 to 1981, characterized by significant declines in production. He distinguished this crisis as one of "underproduction of use values" (scarcity) rather than a capitalist crisis of overproduction, which is marked by an accumulation of unsold commodities and uninvested capital. He also observed similar, though less severe, crises emerging in other post-capitalist societies like Romania, Hungary, Czechoslovakia, and the USSR.

Mandel attributed the immediate cause of the crisis to the "new course" adopted by Edward Gierek's leadership in 1970–71. This program, backed by the Kremlin, aimed for accelerated modernization financed by massive Western borrowing, with the promise of maintaining the living standards of the working people. However, Mandel argued that Gierek's plan dangerously amplified existing disequilibria within the nationalized Polish economy, such as imbalances between economic and social investments, heavy and light industry, and production and distribution. He criticized the absence of socialist democracy and social control over economic life, which allowed bureaucratic cliques to pursue self-interest, engage in corruption through easy access to foreign credits, and foster "gigantomania" in industrial projects. This led to a partial breakdown of planning and distorted productive investments.

Mandel asserted that the summer 1980 strikes, which precipitated the rise of Solidarity, were a "spontaneous response of workers trying to stop this course toward disaster," rather than the cause of the crisis itself. He vehemently refuted the blame placed on workers by the Soviet bureaucracy and its allies, arguing that bureaucratic waste and shortsightedness incurred far greater costs to the Polish economy than the strikes. The international capitalist economic crisis further exacerbated the catastrophic consequences of the Gierek program, which had been predicated on the flawed assumption of sustained capitalist growth. This led to a deterioration of Poland's balance of trade, a surge in foreign debt, and undermined the balance of payments. A long-term structural vulnerability was the persistence of a large private agricultural sector (80% of land) combined with underinvestment and price freezes, leading to stagnation in agricultural production and urban supply crises.

Mandel identified the ultimate cause of the crisis in the "witch's brew of overcentralization and overdecentralization" inherent in the bureaucratic system of management, advocating for "democratically centralized workers self-management" as the only viable solution. He cautioned against imposing the costs of bureaucratic mistakes onto consumers through price increases and layoffs, arguing for extensive workers' and public inspection to expose abuses and privileges. The December 13, 1981, crackdown, in Mandel's view, was a move to implement drastic price increases that would have been impossible with an independent union movement like Solidarity. Mandel actively supported Solidarity, viewing it as a crucial independent workers' movement fighting against bureaucratic dictatorship. He also participated in initiatives supporting the cancellation of Third World debt, linking it to the misery caused by imperialist mechanisms. Mandel's in-depth analysis of the Polish crisis demonstrated his capacity to dissect the internal contradictions of "bureaucratized workers' states" and pinpoint the systemic flaws that lead to economic and social instability. He established a clear cause-and-effect relationship between bureaucratic control and economic dysfunction, linking the crisis directly to the "new course" of bureaucratic management and its inherent "disequilibria" and "gigantomania," exacerbated by the absence of socialist democracy. His assertion that the Solidarity strikes were a response to the crisis, rather than its cause, and that bureaucratic waste was far more damaging, highlighted the agency of the working class in challenging an unsustainable system. This reinforced Mandel's core argument that genuine socialist development requires "democratically centralized workers self-management." The Polish crisis, for Mandel, was a powerful empirical confirmation that bureaucratic rule, even in a non-capitalist context, is inherently unstable and cannot deliver on its promises without the active, democratic participation and control of the working masses. It underscored the necessity of independent workers' organizations to fight for genuine socialist transformation.

II.5. Angola, Mozambique, South Africa: Analysis of Liberation Movements and Post-Independence Trajectories

Ernest Mandel considered the liberation struggles in Mozambique, Angola, and Guinea-Bissau as a "decisive factor" in the fall of fascism in Lisbon. He argued that for two decades, the "center of gravity of the world revolution" had shifted from Western countries to Africa, Asia, and Latin America. During this period, when imperialism was relatively stable in Europe and North America, these struggles played a crucial role in "crystallizing a new revolutionary vanguard" in advanced capitalist countries, thereby enabling the resumption of the struggle for socialist revolution in the West.

Mandel emphasized the "unavoidable duty" for workers and revolutionary youth in Western Europe to "unconditionally support" these struggles until they achieved "unconditional, immediate, and full independence". He specifically called for the release of political prisoners and the immediate withdrawal of Portuguese troops from

Africa. While acknowledging the weakening of imperialist forces in most territories due to the successes of freedom movements, he recognized the "formidable difficulties" faced in South Africa, predicting a "long, complicated, hard, and bitter" struggle that would necessitate "maximum unity" and "skillful planning" within the national movement. Mandel's writings referred to the Popular Movement for the Liberation of Angola (MPLA) and its geopolitical context, including its "proximity to the anti-communist South Africa".

He analyzed the phenomenon of "uneven and combined development" in semi-industrialized countries such as South Africa, India, Brazil, and Mexico. He contended that technological and financial dependence in these nations led to a continuous "draining of resources towards the imperialist metropolises" through unequal exchange, which "obviously hampers long-term economic development". Mandel highlighted the "appalling increase in the misery of the Third World," directly linking it to the deterioration of terms of trade and escalating foreign debt. He actively advocated for the "complete cancellation of the Third World debt" as a crucial act of international solidarity. Mandel's analysis of African liberation movements demonstrated his consistent internationalist perspective, viewing regional struggles as integral components of a broader global revolutionary process. He explicitly linked the success of African liberation movements to the fall of fascism in Europe and the emergence of a new revolutionary vanguard in the West. This implied

a reciprocal relationship: anti-colonial struggles weakened imperialism globally, which in turn created more favorable conditions for socialist movements in advanced capitalist countries. His analysis of "uneven and combined development" in countries like South Africa revealed that even after formal independence, imperialist mechanisms, such as technological and financial dependence and unequal exchange, continued to "drain resources," thereby perpetuating underdevelopment. This suggested that political liberation alone was insufficient without a fundamental economic break from imperialist exploitation. His call for unconditional support and debt cancellation was a direct political implication of this analysis, emphasizing that international solidarity was not merely a moral imperative but a strategic necessity for the global working class.

II.6. Nicaragua: Class Character and Limitations of the Sandinista Revolution

Ernest Mandel's theory of permanent revolution posits that in less developed countries, the full realization of national-democratic tasks—such as national unification, independence from imperialism, and agrarian revolution—is impossible without the conquest of political power by the working class, leading to the destruction of the bourgeois state. He argued against the possibility of "intermediate" state powers existing between the bourgeoisie and the proletariat. Mandel contended that the peasantry, while a vital revolutionary force, is historically compelled to align with either the bourgeoisie or the proletariat, and a victorious revolution necessitates the "hegemony of the pro-letariat".

Despite the Sandinista revolution's anti-imperialist thrust and notable social gains, Mandel's analysis suggested that Nicaragua largely remained a "capitalist state" where bourgeois property relations continued to prevail. He observed that the FSLN, even after eight years, "still refuses to break with imperialism".

The FSLN's "failure to mobilize workers and poor peasants for the creation of a proletarian state," which stemmed from a desire to "co-exist with and conciliate international capital," led to "harsh deprivation" for the masses and consequently "eroded support" for the revolution.

Mandel's framework implied that revolutions that did not culminate in a "full break with the old ruling classes and with international capital" would not be considered "genuine" in the comprehensive sense, as key national-democratic tasks would remain unfulfilled.

He identified the "mixed" economy and "pluralist" democracy in Nicaragua as "contradictory characteristics," reflecting the inherent instability of a regime balancing "antagonistic poles of a capitalist economy vs. the anti-capitalist thrust of the revolution".

While supporting the FSLN's democratic character and its resistance to imperialist aggression, Mandel also highlighted the limitations imposed by this aggression and the imperative to expand elements of direct democracy, enabling the broad masses to determine essential economic and social policies.

Mandel's assessment of the Sandinista revolution in Nicaragua served as a concrete application of his theory of permanent revolution, illustrating the consequences of an incomplete social transformation.

He observed that the Sandinista revolution, despite its anti-imperialist and social gains, was characterized by a "mixed economy" and "pluralist democracy." He argued that Nicaragua remained a "capitalist state" because the FSLN had not made a "full break with imperialism" and had failed to mobilize the masses to create a proletarian state.

This indicated that Mandel moved beyond superficial political labels to analyze the underlying class character of the state. This "failure to mobilize" and "conciliate international capital" directly led to "harsh deprivation" and "eroded support" among the masses. This established a clear causal link: an incomplete social revolution, by failing to fundamentally transform economic relations, undermined its own popular base and rendered it vulnerable.

The Nicaraguan case, for Mandel, confirmed that revolutions in underdeveloped countries must rapidly transition beyond national-democratic tasks to socialist ones, or they risk stagnation, internal contradictions, and ultimately defeat or reversal.

It underscored the "all or nothing" logic of permanent revolution in the imperialist epoch, where a "half-way" revolution is inherently unstable.

Comparative Table of Country-Specific Critiques and Alternatives

Country/Movement	Key System Characteristics (as analyzed by Mandel)	Mandel's Main Critiques	Mandel's Proposed Alternatives/Solutions
Yugoslavia	Workers' self-management, extensive market mechanisms, one-party political monopoly.	Increasing social inequality, abdication of central planning, market mechanisms reproducing capitalist contradictions, bureaucracy at local/managerial levels, vague theory of self-management.	Democratic centralization with a priori central planning, market mechanisms limited to consumer goods, federal central body of workers' councils.
China	"Deformed revolution" with peasant army, heavily bureaucratized party/state, "Cultural Revolution" as intra-bureaucratic conflict, agricultural policies leading to social differentiation.	Overestimation of peasant sacrifice, lack of genuine workers' councils, ideological distortions (Mao cult, subjective definition of "capitalist"), bureaucracy's resilience in co-opting mass movements, economic setbacks from flawed policies.	Genuine workers' power based on democratically elected councils (Soviets), widest proletarian democracy, abolition of income inequality, international extension of revolution.
Cuba	State ownership, central planning (Budgetary Finance System - BFS), anti-imperialist stance, rapid social progress.	Danger of bureaucracy from absence of workers' democracy at national level, potential for market mechanisms to reproduce underdevelopment if not consciously subordinated to plan.	Genuine workers' management at enterprise level, workers' democracy at state level, national congress of workers' committees, centralized investments with democratically established priorities.
Poland	Post-capitalist society with bureaucratic management, large private agricultural sector, reliance on Western borrowing.	Crisis of underproduction, bureaucratic "gigantomania" and disequilibria, absence of socialist democracy, bureaucratic waste exceeding strike costs, negative impact of international capitalist crisis.	Democratically centralized workers' self-management, extensive workers' and public inspection, rejection of price increases/layoffs to cover bureaucratic mistakes.
Angola, Mozambique, South Africa	Liberation struggles against colonialism/apartheid, post-independence semi-industrialization with technological/financial dependence.	Continued "draining of resources" by imperialist mechanisms (unequal exchange), perpetuation of misery in the Third World despite political independence.	Unconditional support from Western workers, complete cancellation of Third World debt, international solidarity to counter imperialist exploitation.
Nicaragua	Sandinista revolution with anti-imperialist thrust and social gains, but mixed economy and pluralist democracy.	Failure to break fully with imperialism, refusal to create a proletarian state, conciliation with international capital leading to deprivation and eroded popular support.	Conquest of political power by working class, destruction of bourgeois state, establishment of proletarian hegemony, rapid transition to socialist tasks.

III. Late-Career Theoretical Refinements and Self-Criticisms

Ernest Mandel's intellectual journey was marked by a continuous process of theoretical development and critical self-reflection, particularly evident in his later career as he grappled with evolving global capitalism and the transformations within post-capitalist states.

III.1. Evolution of Long Wave Theory and Economic Predictions

Mandel significantly contributed to Marxist economic theory through his development of the concepts of "neo-capitalism" and later, "late capitalism," which described the post-World War II epoch of capitalist growth, technological innovation, and increased state intervention. Central to this framework was his revival and elaboration of "long waves" of capitalist expansion and contraction, a concept initially identified by Nikolai Kondratiev. These waves typically involved approximately 25-30 years of economic expansion, driven by investment in new technology and increased capital accumulation, followed by a similar period of downswing characterized by slumping profits and slower economic growth.

A notable aspect of Mandel's intellectual rigor was his capacity for self-criticism. He acknowledged that he had initially "mistakenly clung to the idea, not borne out by the facts, of an irreversible stagnation of the economy shortly after the Second World War". This error compelled him to recognize the necessity of studying a "third type of rhythm"—beyond the short-term industrial cycle and the system's overall life cycle—to fully grasp capitalism's dynamics, leading to his refined long wave theory.

Mandel's approach to predicting capitalist breakdown was nuanced, distinguishing him from those who mechanistically forecast capitalism's immediate collapse. Instead, he aimed to identify the complex interplay of contemporary economic and class forces in real time. For instance, in his 1977 work The Second Slump, he presciently identified a new instability in global banking that would have profound consequences decades later, as seen in the 2008 financial crisis. He observed that large corporations were increasingly able to borrow from banks while obscuring their accounts, and that a decline in the competence of bank officials, coupled with intensified competition, led banks to undertake greater risks. He also noted a trend towards central banks underwriting this reckless lending, which opened the prospect of increasingly dangerous financial crises.

Mandel's method involved applying Marxist economic categories to current problems, illuminated by contemporary data, rather than relying solely on textual citations from Das Kapital. He broke with the mechanical determinism that had influenced some interpretations of Marx, reaffirming Marx's original insight that the capitalist system is determined by a dialectical interplay of real forces. Consequently, Mandel, like Marx, eschewed mono-causal explanations for capitalist instability and breakdown. He maintained that the capitalist economic system is inherently entropic and susceptible to existential disruption due to its internal inconsistencies. He theorized that crisis is structurally embedded in the system, where excessive global capital accumulation eventually reduces the average rate of profit to a point where the extra productivity from new technical investments becomes insufficient to cover their cost. This illustrates a commitment to empirical validation and a non-deterministic understanding of capitalist development.

III.2. Reassessment of Stalinism and the Collapse of the Soviet Union

Ernest Mandel consistently rejected the theory of "state capitalism" as applied to the Soviet Union and other post-capitalist states. For him, the defining characteristic of capitalism was the generalization of commodity production and competition between individual capitals. He argued that the Soviet economy, with its state ownership of major means of production, centralized planning, and absence of a market for capital or labor-power, was fundamentally non-capitalist. Instead, he defined Soviet society as a "transitional society" between capitalism and socialism, albeit one severely deformed by a privileged bureaucracy.

Mandel's analysis of the Soviet bureaucracy was crucial. He defined it as "the sum total of all materially privileged elements and layers which are not private owners of the means of production". He argued that while the bureaucracy's material self-interest was the primary instrument for plan realization, there was no economic mechanism to ensure this self-interest aligned with the

optimization of economic growth, especially after a certain threshold of industrialization. This inherent conflict led to enormous distortions and waste in the planning process, such as hiding reserves, transmitting false information, and producing low-quality outputs. He stressed that the bureaucracy's power stemmed from the decline of independent mass activity and that its blows against bourgeois forces often occurred after it had already weakened the Soviet Union and its proletariat, resulting in unnecessary losses and hindering progress towards a classless society.

Despite his long-standing critique of the Soviet bureaucracy, Mandel initially expressed skepticism about the possibility of a short-term capitalist restoration in the USSR and other bureaucratized workers' states after 1989. In October 1989, he believed the primary conflict was between the bureaucracy and the toiling masses, and that the convergence of forces would be insufficient to impose capitalist restoration in the short or medium term. In February 1990, he further elaborated, describing events in East Germany and Czechoslovakia as the "beginning of a revolutionary movement" developing under "exceptionally favourable international conditions," asserting that "a short-term restoration of capitalism is completely impossible – even the capitalists do not want it".

However, the subsequent collapse of these states and the widespread reintroduction of capitalism necessitated a reassessment. While some critics claimed Mandel's theory of the inconceivability of capitalist restoration proved wrong, his broader framework provided tools to understand the unfolding events. Mandel later argued that the collapse was possible because "power was usurped by a bureaucracy whose political base disintegrated". He explained that the growing and conflictual decomposition of the bureaucracy itself accelerated the disintegration of Soviet society. Mandel's analysis of the bureaucracy's inherent instability was confirmed by the collapse, but the speed and extent of capitalist restoration challenged his short-term predictions. This demonstrated that while the bureaucracy was not a ruling class in the traditional Marxist sense, its internal contradictions and inability to effectively manage the economy could indeed pave the way for a return to capitalism under specific historical conditions. He warned that if the Soviet economy were privatized, the USSR would likely become a "Third World country," not a developed capitalist one, leading to mass resistance and repression.

III.3. Creative Marxism vs. Dogmatism

Ernest Mandel's intellectual approach was fundamentally rooted in a commitment to creative Marxism, actively resisting dogmatism within socialist thought. This was evident in his engagement with various theoretical debates, such as his critique of Althusserianism, where he argued against the notion of an "epistemological break" in Marx's thought, emphasizing instead a continuous "evolution". His co-authored book Offener Marxismus. Ein Gespräch über Dogmen, Orthodoxie und die Häresie der Realität (Open Marxism: A Discussion about Doctrines, Orthodoxy and the Heresy of Reality) explicitly positioned him against the "dogmatism of Marxism-Leninism," advocating for an "openness to praxis and history".

Mandel consistently championed unlimited political democracy and freedom of the press as indispensable for the development of socialist society. He argued that any restriction on press freedom, even for reasons of "objectivity" or "responsibility," inherently undermines it, as such criteria are subjective and can lead to censorship. He aligned with Marx's polemics against censorship, viewing "irresponsible," "subjective" reporting, and "disinformation" as lesser evils than censorship itself.

For Mandel, building socialism was a process of "successive, often contradictory experiments," where mistakes were inevitable. The key, he believed, was the ability to limit and quickly correct these errors, which necessitated the "fullest expression of minority counterproposals" and unlimited political democracy. He rejected the idea of infallibility, asserting that truth is "never final" and can only be discovered through the "fullest possible debate and freedom of opinion". He famously articulated the "right of error for majorities," emphasizing the need and capacity for self-education among the toilers through trial-and-error and the confrontation of opposing ideas. Mandel's advocacy for intellectual freedom was central to preventing Marxism from becoming a sterile dogma. His insistence that truth is discovered through open debate, and that even "wrong ideas" must be expressed to allow for self-correction, directly challenged the authoritarian tendencies seen in Stalinist and Maoist regimes. This approach underscored his belief that a vibrant, evolving Marxist theory requires constant engagement with new facts and scientific considerations, rather than rigid adherence to preconceived schemas.

IV. Institutional and Organizational Questions for Socialist Transformation

Ernest Mandel's theoretical contributions extended deeply into the practical questions of building a socialist society, particularly concerning its institutional and organizational foundations. He consistently emphasized that genuine socialist transformation required specific democratic structures to prevent bureaucratic degeneration and ensure authentic workers' power.

IV.1. Socialist Democracy, Multi-Party Systems, and Press Freedom

Mandel was a staunch advocate for unlimited political democracy during the transition from capitalism to communism, asserting that collective social power and individual rights are complementary and essential for a communist society. He unequivocally supported multi-party, multi-platform democracy, which he believed could not be realized without unlimited freedom of the press.

His detailed program for press freedom included guaranteeing every civilian group access to printing presses and media, strictly proportional to the support they could mobilize, verified by signatures, sales, or audience metrics. He proposed quantitative examples, such as 20,000 people gaining the right to publish a daily paper, or lesser numbers for weeklies or monthlies. The only constraint on this freedom, he argued, should be material resources, allocated by a nationwide body like a congress of workers' and popular councils. However, media producers could not be forced to exceed a democratically decided workload. Mandel explicitly stated that this material limitation did not restrict the freedom of individuals to express their ideas, rejecting any restriction based on "objectivity," "fairness," or "responsibility" as potential censorship.

Mandel fundamentally believed that limiting press freedom hindered the construction of socialism because there are no definitive "rules" or "laws" about its nature; society during this period is a "huge laboratory of successive, often contradictory experiments," making mistakes inevitable. The capacity to limit and quickly correct these mistakes necessitated the fullest expression of minority counterproposals, which in turn required unlimited political democracy and press freedom. He rejected the notion of infallibility, aligning with Engels's view that "socialist science" cannot develop without the "fullest freedom of movement". He referenced Rosa Luxemburg's prophecy that restricting political freedoms to a single-party system would lead to the disappearance of political life from the Soviets, leaving only bureaucracy as an active factor. Mandel's view of robust democratic freedoms as indispensable for genuine socialist construction and a safeguard against bureaucracy was a cornerstone of his theoretical framework. He argued that democracy was not a luxury to be granted after socialism was achieved, but a necessary condition for its very realization. This perspective directly challenged the authoritarian practices of existing "socialist" states and underscored his commitment to a truly emancipatory political system.

IV.2. Workers' Councils, Self-Management, and Economic Freedom

Mandel asserted that the extension of human rights and freedom to the economic sphere was entirely complementary with unlimited press freedom. He argued that economic freedom for producers to control their lives and working conditions depended on suppressing private ownership of large means of production and exchange, and emancipation from market laws, profit motives, and capital accumulation. It also hinged on their right and power to escape "either state despotism or market despotism" and to freely, collectively, and consciously decide what to produce, how to produce, and how to distribute a significant part of the output.

Recognizing that producer/consumers are not homogeneous in their interests or understanding, Mandel acknowledged that differences of opinion about priorities would be unavoidable. He contended that if multi-party, multi-platform democracy and press freedom were restricted, sectors of the working class would be restricted in their economic freedom. Economic freedom at macro-economic and macro-social levels, he argued, required the possibility for workers to choose among alternative proposals for economic development and coherent development plans, which could not be realized without the fullest freedom of discussion and press.

Mandel's vision of democratically centralized self-management was not merely theoretical; it was a practical blueprint for organizing a post-capitalist society. He envisioned dozens, if not hundreds, of democratically elected and functioning self-administration bodies, with nearly everyone participating in several. A material precondition for generalized self-management and self-administration, he noted, was a radical reduction of the workday and workweek for all. Mandel's vision linked political freedoms with economic self-determination for the working class. He understood that without genuine control over the means and processes of production, political liberties could remain superficial. This emphasis on economic freedom, manifested through self-management and collective decision-making, was designed to prevent the emergence of new forms of exploitation, whether by a state bureaucracy or residual market forces.

IV.3. The Role of the Revolutionary Party and Democratic Centralism

Mandel viewed the revolutionary party as an indispensable "subjective factor" for guiding mass movements towards socialist transformation. He argued that radical change was possible only during "waves of unrest" when capitalism's contradictions generated mass anger and protest. During such periods, a revolutionary party should aim to draw ever larger groups into political action and propose anti-capitalist demands, understanding revolution as a process of interaction between organized action and spontaneous movement.

His perspective on internal party democracy was robust. He emphasized the necessity of a party where members enjoyed the "actual right to define the direction of the party policy," including "freedom of criticism and intellectual struggle." He explicitly rejected the notion that Bolshevism did not tolerate factions, stating that the "history of Bolshevism is a history of the struggle of factions". He also advocated for the non-prohibition of factions, even if they were considered "bad," arguing that their banning was "a cure worse than the illness".

Mandel consistently rejected the idea of a single-party monopoly as a necessary precondition or feature of workers' power, stating that no theoretical or programmatic document of Marx, Engels, Lenin, or Trotsky ever proposed such a system. He argued that classes are heterogeneous and arrive at solutions through an inner struggle of tendencies, groups, and parties. He believed that the artificial administrative suppression of parties, even those reflecting currents among the masses, increased dangers rather than reducing them, and that reformist influence would persist and should be combatted through ideological struggle rather than repression.

A guiding principle for Mandel from his earliest days in the European Trotskyist movement was the necessity of "mergers and fusions" of political tendencies within the working-class movement to build a mass international. This strategy was rooted in the history of the Russian Revolution and the Bolshevik party prior to Stalinism, and the Trotskyist Left Opposition's struggle against Stalinism. Mandel's approach sought to reconcile the need for organized leadership with the imperative of mass democratic participation. He understood that while spontaneous mass movements were crucial, they required a conscious, programmatic vanguard to achieve lasting revolutionary change. His strong advocacy for internal party democracy and the right to factions demonstrated his conviction that the revolutionary party itself must embody the democratic principles it seeks to implement in society, thereby serving as a safeguard against its own bureaucratization.

IV.4. International Coordination vs. National Autonomy in the Fourth International

Mandel, as a leading figure of the Fourth International, consistently emphasized the imperative of international organization for the proletariat. He argued that "without the international organisation of the proletariat, the co-ordination and indeed the understanding of the international process of class struggle, the revolution will be more difficult, the defeats more heavy". This perspective underscored the belief that the global nature of capitalism necessitated a globally coordinated revolutionary response.

The Fourth International, under Mandel's influence, aimed to tackle the political problems of worldwide class struggle collectively, thinking about and solving problems encountered in individual countries together. This vision implied a degree of international coordination that would guide national sections, ensuring a unified strategy against global capitalism and bureaucratic forces.

However, the practical implementation of international coordination also brought forth questions of national autonomy. While the ideal was a "world party" that could define and plan internationally coordinated campaigns, the reality often involved national organizational fragmentation. Mandel acknowledged that the Fourth International had, at times, underestimated the importance of nationalism and its influence within the working class. He believed that the effect of this national organizational fragmentation could undermine the ability to construct genuine international perspectives. The imperative of internationalism, for Mandel, was not merely an abstract principle but a practical necessity for overcoming capitalist and bureaucratic challenges. He recognized that the "periodically explosive nature of the contradictions between the productive forces and the capitalist relations of production" manifested through "outbreaks of working class struggles which paralyse the functioning of the capitalist system," and that these required an international response. This understanding highlighted the continuous tension and dialectical relationship between the global nature of class struggle and the national specificities of revolutionary movements, demanding flexible yet principled international coordination.

Conclusion

Ernest Mandel's intellectual and political contributions represent a profound and enduring legacy within Marxist thought. His work consistently demonstrated a commitment to applying and creatively developing historical materialism to understand the complexities of the 20th century.

His personal engagements, particularly with figures like Che Guevara, underscored his belief in the vital interplay between theoretical rigor and revolutionary practice. These interactions revealed his conviction that economic transformation, especially in underdeveloped nations, must be consciously planned and democratically controlled to avoid the pitfalls of market logic and bureaucratic deformation.

Mandel's detailed country-specific analyses, from Yugoslavia's market socialism to China's Cultural Revolution, Poland's economic crisis, and liberation movements in Africa and Latin America, consistently highlighted the systemic contradictions of "bureaucratized workers' states" and the inherent instability of incomplete revolutions. He meticulously demonstrated how the absence of genuine workers' democracy and the persistence of bureaucratic interests led to economic inefficiencies, social inequalities, and ultimately, vulnerability to internal and external pressures. His analyses consistently pointed to the necessity of a "full break" with old ruling classes and international capital, arguing that partial transformations inevitably lead to stagnation or reversal.

In his late-career theoretical refinements, Mandel exhibited a remarkable capacity for self-criticism, as seen in his evolution of the long wave theory. His nuanced understanding of capitalist dynamics, which eschewed mechanistic collapse predictions in favor of a dialectical analysis of structural contradictions, reflected a commitment to empirical grounding and intellectual honesty. His persistent critique of Stalinism, defining Soviet society as a bureaucratically deformed transitional state rather than "state capitalist," provided a framework for understanding its eventual collapse, even if the speed of capitalist restoration challenged his short-term predictions. His advocacy for "Open Marxism" and unlimited democratic freedoms underscored his belief that Marxism must remain a living, evolving science, constantly refined through open debate and the "right to be wrong."

Finally, Mandel's perspectives on institutional and organizational questions for socialist transformation were rooted in a deep commitment to genuine workers' democracy. He championed multi-party systems, unrestricted press freedom, and robust workers' councils as indispensable safeguards against bureaucracy and essential for the self-emancipation of the working class. He sought to balance the necessity of a revolutionary vanguard party with the imperative of mass self-activity and internal party democracy, recognizing that the international nature of capitalism demanded a coordinated global revolutionary movement.

In sum, Ernest Mandel's analytical framework remains highly relevant for understanding global capitalism, the challenges of post-capitalist societies, and the ongoing struggle for a genuinely democratic and international socialist future. His work serves as a testament to the power of a non-dogmatic, critically engaged Marxist perspective in navigating complex historical processes and informing revolutionary practice.

Part Two

Responding to the AWL's Distortions of Ernest Mandel

Sectarian Distortions and Historical Falsification

Ernest Mandel died 30 years ago this week. The Alliance for Workers' Liberty recently republished its open letter to Ernest Mandel. As we explained earlier this month, Sean Matgamna's open letter is a work of staggering misrepresentation and bad faith

*"Matgamna's method demonstrated such **profound bad faith** that meaningful debate became virtually impossible. Major sections of his argumentation were based on **systematic and deliberate deformation of the positions it polemicizes against**, taking forms **so outrageous and slanderous that it borders on the grotesque**, effectively creating **straw men** that replaced real positions. He attributed views that Mandel and the Fourth International (FI) explicitly rejected."*

The AWL's open letter is not well cited. We have created two reports outlining Mandel's views (Ernest Mandel's Evolving Perspectives on 20th Century Socialism and Capitalism, and Ernest Mandel: Some of his Contributions to Marxist Theory and Revolutionary Practice), and our reply to the AWL is based on what we have found. Of course, Mandel's work spans many languages, and not all his writings are easily available in English. Therefore, we start this series with an important caveat: we doubt that the AWL's polemic is well-founded on any points, but we encourage them to back up their claims; we would be delighted to update our understanding of the evolution of Mandel's thinking.

A Sectarian Attack Built on False Premises

Sean Matgamna's open letter to Ernest Mandel, titled "Trotskyism after the collapse of Stalinism," presents itself as a serious critique of post-war Trotskyism. However, a careful examination of the historical record reveals something far more troubling: a systematic distortion of facts so egregious that it undermines the entire credibility of the Alliance for Workers' Liberty's position.

Matgamna opens his letter with a sweeping condemnation: "The collapse of the USSR shows conclusively that your version of 'Trotskyism' was radically wrong, false, and disorienting." He characterizes Mandel as "the representative leader of post-Trotsky 'Trotskyism'" who has "performed the typical 'ideological' work of post-Trotsky 'Trotskyism' — rationalising 'the historic process'."

But the most serious accusation comes when Matgamna claims that Mandel and his tendency "identified this development with the 'World Revolution' of the proletariat" and "automatically took their side against imperialism, and thus, for example, for the USSR against the German workers in the workers' revolt in East Germany in 1953."

This final charge—that Ernest Mandel and the Fourth International supported the USSR against East German workers in 1953—forms the centerpiece of Matgamna's attack on Mandel's anti-Stalinist credentials. If true, it would indeed represent a fundamental betrayal of revolutionary principles. There is only one problem: as far as we can see from the materials available, **it**

is completely and demonstrably false.

The Smoking Gun: What Really Happened in 1953

The historical record on the Fourth International's position regarding the 1953 East German uprising is unambiguous and readily available to any serious researcher. Far from supporting Soviet intervention, the documentary evidence shows the exact opposite.

The FI unequivocally supported the workers' uprising in East Germany in June 1953. The International Secretariat (IS) of the <u>Fourth International</u> issued a declaration hailing the East Berlin uprising as the first salvo of the political revolution in the East.

The Fourth International's position was not one of equivocation or diplomatic neutrality. The FI characterized it as a revolutionary movement and endorsed the workers' demands, specifically calling for the restoration of freely elected workers' councils. Moreover, the FI reiterated its long-standing call for the withdrawal of all occupation troops from Germany, encompassing Soviet forces in the East, as well as American, British, and French troops in the West.

Most damning to Matgamna's accusation is the Fourth International's clear condemnation of Soviet actions: The intervention of Soviet occupation forces to militarily suppress the workers was a significant factor in the FI's analysis, as it marked the initial instance of military force being used against

workers within the Soviet bloc's periphery.

This was not an isolated position but flowed directly from the Fourth International's broader program for the Eastern European states. This programme included crucial demands such as: Freedom of political and trade union organization, Workers' armament, and Abolition of privileges for the bureaucratic caste.

A Pattern of Historical Vindication

The Fourth International's principled stance in 1953 was not an accident but reflected a consistent analysis that proved remarkably prescient. The FI viewed later events, such as the Poznań uprising in 1956 and the Hungarian Revolution of 1956, as confirming its perspectives. The Polish movement's half-victory was attributed to the centrist current of Gomulka, which provided an alternative leadership, while the Hungarian uprising's tragic defeat was linked to an unfavourable balance of forces and the absence of mass movements in the USSR itself. The rise of Solidarnosc in 1980 in Poland was also seen as a powerful confirmation of the FI's long-standing analysis and demands for political revolution and workers' self-organization in the region.

Each of these subsequent events validated the Fourth International's analysis that bureaucratic states faced inevitable internal contradictions that would manifest in worker uprisings demanding genuine democracy. Far from supporting the Soviet bureaucracy against workers, the Fourth International consistently predicted and supported such movements.

The Credibility Crisis: When Central Claims Collapse

When a political critique is built around a central factual claim that proves to be entirely false, it raises serious questions about the methodology and credibility of the entire analysis. Matgamna's letter is not based on a minor historical misunderstanding or a difference of interpretation—it rests on a fundamental falsification of the historical record.

This falsification is particularly egregious because the 1953 East German uprising represents a crucial test of any organization's anti-Stalinist credentials. It was the first major worker uprising against Stalinist rule, and how revolutionary organizations responded revealed their true character. The Fourth International passed this test with flying colors, while Matgamna's account inverts reality entirely.

The implications extend far beyond a single historical event. If Matgamna is willing to make such a demonstrably false claim about something as well-documented as the Fourth International's 1953 position, what confidence can we have in his characterization of Mandel's positions on other complex issues?

Sectarian Methodology: Caricature Over Analysis

Matgamna's false claim about 1953 reveals a broader methodological problem that runs throughout his letter. Rather than engaging seriously with Mandel's actual positions, he consistently presents caricatures designed to serve his sectarian purposes.

Consider how Matgamna characterizes Mandel's theoretical framework: "You, comrade Mandel, have personified the characteristic mixture of post-Trotsky 'Trotskyism': recognition of currents like Titoism, Castroism and Maoism as 'revolutionary' and adaptation to them, while attempting to explain your current political preconceptions and perspectives in terms of the politics of Lenin and Trotsky."

This formulation—recognition as revolutionary and adaptation to them—fundamentally misrepresents Mandel's sophisticated analysis of these movements. As we shall demonstrate in subsequent articles, Mandel developed nuanced critiques of the bureaucratic deformations in Yugoslavia, Cuba, and China while maintaining support for anti-imperialist struggle. This position of critical solidarity is precisely the opposite of the uncritical adaptation that Matgamna alleges.

Similarly, when Matgamna claims that the majority of the forces making up post-Trotsky Trotskyism followed Mandel in seeing the Stalinist states as degenerated or deformed 'workers' states', *in advance of and superior to capitalism,* he presents this as evidence of capitulation to Stalinism. In reality, the degenerated workers' state analysis was developed precisely as a tool for understanding how to fight against Stalinist bureaucracy while defending the social gains of the revolution.

The Stakes of Historical Accuracy

The falsification of Mandel's 1953 position is not merely an academic error—it represents a fundamental distortion of the political landscape of the 20th century left. Matgamna's letter attempts to rewrite history to present the AWL's sectarian positions as the only authentic continuation of Trotskyist tradition, while dismissing more sophisticated analyses as "adaptations" to Stalinism.

This methodology—creating "straw dolls" out of complex positions and then attacking these caricatures—serves to obscure rather than illuminate the real issues facing revolutionary socialists. When Matgamna writes that "It is time to face up to that, comrade Mandel — high time, if the cadres of 'Trotskyism' are now to be preserved as revolutionaries," he presents himself as defending revolutionary orthodoxy. But his own falsification of the historical record suggests that the AWL's version of "orthodox Trotskyism" requires systematic distortion to sustain itself.

The International Context: Critical Solidarity vs. Sectarian Dogma Dresses As 'Purity'

Matgamna's letter reflects a broader problem within sectarian Trotskyist organizations: the inability to develop sophisticated analyses of complex revolutionary processes that don't fit neat theoretical categories. The Fourth International under Mandel's leadership faced the challenge of analyzing post-war revolutions led by non-Trotskyist forces in a world where capitalism had stabilized in the advanced countries while revolutionary movements emerged in the colonial world.

Rather than retreating into sectarian purity, Mandel and the Fourth International developed what they called critical solidarity—unconditional support for anti-imperialist struggles combined with consistent criticism of bureaucratic methods and advocacy for genuine workers' democracy. This approach allowed them to maintain revolutionary principles while engaging with the actual dynamics of 20th-century revolutionary movements.

The AWL's approach, by contrast, appears to require a kind of theoretical dogma that can only be maintained by systematically misrepresenting more nuanced positions. When reality doesn't conform to sectarian formulas, the solution is apparently to distort reality rather than develop more sophisticated analysis.

Conclusion: The Foundation Crumbles

Sean Matgamna's open letter to Ernest Mandel presents itself as a serious reckoning with the failures of post-war Trotskyism. However, when its central factual claim—that Mandel supported the USSR against East German workers in 1953—proves to be entirely false, the entire edifice collapses.

This is not a minor error or a difference of interpretation. It is a fundamental falsification that reveals the

AWL's methodology: rather than engaging seriously with Mandel's actual positions, they create caricatures that serve their sectarian purposes and then attack these "straw dolls" as if they were addressing real political questions.

The historical record shows that on the crucial test of the 1953 East German uprising, Ernest Mandel and the Fourth International took the most principled anti-Stalinist position possible—unequivocal support for the workers against Soviet military intervention. This position flowed from a consistent analysis that proved remarkably prescient, correctly predicting the series of worker uprisings that would shake the Eastern bloc over the following decades.

When an organization's critique is built on such demonstrable falsehoods, serious revolutionaries must ask: what other distortions lie beneath the surface? In the subsequent parts of this response, we will systematically examine Matgamna's other major claims and demonstrate that the pattern of misrepresentation revealed in the 1953 case extends throughout his analysis.

The choice facing contemporary socialists is clear: we can accept the AWL's sectarian distortions and retreat into theoretical purism, or we can learn from Mandel's example of principled engagement with complex revolutionary realities. The historical record suggests that Mandel's approach, whatever its limitations, offered a far more sophisticated and ultimately more revolutionary path than the AWL's sectarian alternative.

The falsification of the 1953 record is not just an attack on Ernest Mandel—it is an attack on the possibility of developing living, creative Marxist analysis in the face of complex historical realities. That is why exposing this distortion is crucial for anyone serious about revolutionary politics in the 21st century.

Postscript: The Distortion Mechanism

A careful examination of how Matgamna constructs his false accusation reveals the systematic methodology behind AWL distortions. The chain of misrepresentation works as follows:

First, Matgamna conflates Michel Pablo's position with Ernest Mandel's, assuming that because Pablo held a particular view, Mandel necessarily shared it. This guilt-by-association approach ignores the complex internal debates within the Fourth International and Mandel's own evolving positions.

Second, Matgamna distorts even Pablo's position. While Pablo indeed called for the withdrawal of both Soviet and Western occupation forces from Germany (not just Soviet forces), Matgamna characterizes this as refusing to call for Russian withdrawal—a fundamental misrepresentation. The Fourth International's position was actually more radical than calling for Soviet withdrawal alone: it demanded the end of all foreign military occupation.

The historical record confirms this principled stance. The demand for the withdrawal of all foreign troops, including Russian troops, from Germany was indeed adopted by the International Executive Committee (CEI) in June 1946. This marked the first time this specific demand was officially included in the International's resolutions. The Fourth International explicitly stated it would in no way abandon this slogan and would campaign for the immediate departure of occupation troops in every occupied country.

This position emerged from extensive internal debate and theoretical development. While discussions about Red Army occupation had been ongoing since 1945, the International Executive Committee noted in January 1945 that amendments highlighting the role assumed by the Red Army in these countries, hindering any revolutionary development, and envisaging the application of the slogan of immediate withdrawal of these troops, were not adopted at that earlier point. This illustrates the internal difficulty in reaching a unified and clear stance on challenging Soviet actions directly.

By June 1946, however, the newly elected International Executive Committee adopted a resolution titled "Au sujet des territoires occupés" (Concerning the occupied territories), which for the first time incorporated the demand for the withdrawal of all foreign armies, including the Red Army, from all occupied territories. The Fourth International recognized the reactionary nature of the Soviet occupation, noting that the Soviet bureaucracy was even seen applying forced labor to the German proletariat.

The demand for troop withdrawal was firmly rooted in the Fourth International's principled commitment to the right of peoples to self-determination. It was part of a broader denunciation of monstrous plans of plunder and rapine concerning the fate of the defeated countries, and first and foremost Germany, elaborated by the diplomats of the 'allied' imperialist bourgeoisie and the Stalinist bureaucracy.

Third, from this double distortion, Matgamna extrapolates a sweeping characterization: that the FI backs the USSR against Western imperialism in every conflict. This represents a complete inversion of the Fourth International's actual position, which opposed both Soviet bureaucracy and Western imperialism from as early as 1946.

The irony is remarkable: Matgamna attacks the Fourth International for being "pro-USSR" precisely because they took a more thoroughgoing anti-imperialist position than he would accept. Their call for the withdrawal of all occupation forces—Soviet, American, British, and French—was more principled than demanding only Soviet withdrawal, which would have left Germany under Western military control.

The Fourth International's evolving analysis shows serious theoretical development, not capitulation. Despite internal debates—with groups like the British Revolutionary Communist Party arguing that Eastern European countries had already become bureaucratized workers' states and should be defended against Western imperialism—the Second World Congress in

1948 rejected amendments from the RCP on this matter and maintained a more critical analysis. Full theoretical consensus on characterizing them as deformed workers' states was not reached until the Third World Congress in 1951, showing careful theoretical development rather than rushed accommodation.

This parallels contemporary debates, where comrades in the tradition of the Fourth International calling for the abolition of NATO are attacked as "pro-Russian" (and sometimes even pro-NATO), despite taking a position that opposes all imperialist military blocs. The sectarian mind cannot grasp that genuine anti-imperialism means opposing all imperial powers, not just selecting one's preferred camp.

Matgamna's methodology—conflation, distortion, and extrapolation—reveals how sectarian organizations manufacture "scandals" to attack more sophisticated positions. When the historical record doesn't support their narrative, they systematically twist it until it appears to do so. This is not honest political debate but ideological fabrication in service of sectarian warfare.

Straw Dolls and
the Crisis Theory Fabrication

Sean Matgamna's open letter to Ernest Mandel represents a particularly insidious form of sectarian polemic: the systematic construction of "straw dolls" that bear little resemblance to the actual positions they purport to critique. When revolutionary organizations engage in such methods, they poison the well of theoretical debate and make genuine advancement of Marxist theory impossible. Our task in this second article is to expose these distortions by contrasting Matgamna's caricatures with Mandel's actual theoretical positions, documented in his extensive published works and contemporary debates.

The Central Claim: A Fundamental Misunderstanding

Matgamna's central thesis is clear: "The collapse of the USSR shows conclusively that your version of 'Trotskyism' was radically wrong, false, and disorienting." This argument rests on a fundamental misunderstanding of what Trotskyist theory actually predicted about the fate of the Soviet Union.

Matgamna presents the collapse of the USSR as somehow refuting Mandel's theoretical framework. But this turns the actual Trotskyist analysis on its head. The Fourth International consistently maintained that without political revolution by the working class, bureaucratically deformed states remained vulnerable to capitalist restoration.

In his response to the British SWP during the crisis period of 1991, Mandel made clear that capitalist restoration would represent "a major victory for world imperialism" requiring "major defeats on the working class." The collapse of 1991 represented precisely the outcome that Trotskyist theory had long warned against when genuine workers' democracy failed to emerge.

The "Periphery Fallacy" Demolished

One of Matgamna's most persistent distortions concerns the supposed "periphery fallacy"—the claim that Mandel relied primarily on revolutionary movements at the "periphery" rather than focusing on class struggle in advanced capitalist countries. The documentary evidence from the 1967 debate with Ted Knight and Peter Taaffe completely demolishes this straw doll.

Mandel's actual position in 1967 was unambiguous: "the key to the overthrow of capitalism is in the struggle between labour and capital in the centres of capitalism." While acknowledging that imperialism could be weakened by revolutionary developments in backward countries, this was strategic support designed to facilitate revolution in advanced countries.

Mandel drew a historical parallel to the Bolsheviks, noting that they made revolution in backward Russia not primarily to build socialism there, but to weaken world capitalism and facilitate revolution in imperialist countries. He asked whether the American working class had contributed as much to weakening American imperialism as the Vietnamese revolution.

This strategic framework recognized that supporting anti-imperialist struggles was justified because it struck at the root of the world imperialist system while serving to heighten revolutionary consciousness in Western Europe. Far from escaping into peripheral adventures, Mandel saw this as concrete internationalist strategy.

Significantly, this <u>1967 debate</u> shows that similar arguments to Matgamna's were already being made by Ted Knight and Peter Taaffe—both of whom later broke from the Fourth International. This reveals the recurring pattern of sectarian critique that substitutes mechanical formulas for dialectical analysis.

The Crisis Theory Fabrication

One of Matgamna's most egregious distortions concerns Mandel's crisis theory. He suggests that Mandel lacked a coherent definition of capitalist crisis or relied on subjective assessments. The documentary evidence completely refutes this caricature.

Mandel explicitly defined revolutionary crisis and provided rigorous analysis grounded in Marx's method. He stated that the capitalist system had been in crisis since 1914-1917 and provided historical instances to illustrate this analysis.

Far from being subjective, Mandel's crisis theory was grounded in rigorous analysis of capitalism's structural contradictions. He devoted his masterwork "Late Capitalism" to analyzing the contradictions between the growth of productive forces and capitalist relations of production.

Mandel's approach was explicitly multicausal, seeking to develop crisis theory based on Marx's works. This sophisticated theoretical framework involved studying multiple variables across different sectors and demonstrated methodological rigor that bears no resemblance to Matgamna's straw doll characterization.

The "Adaptation" Caricature Exposed

Matgamna characterizes Mandel's approach as "recognition of currents like Titoism, Castroism and Maoism as 'revolutionary' and adaptation to them." This represents perhaps the most significant distortion in his entire letter, as it completely inverts the Fourth International's actual strategic framework.

The documentary evidence reveals that Mandel advocated what he explicitly called "unity of action" combined with "merciless ideological struggle." This was not uncritical adaptation but a sophisticated strategic approach rooted in Marxist united front tactics.

Mandel drew an analogy to participating in strikes alongside workers of various ideological tendencies because without unity of action of the whole working class, there could never be socialist revolution in advanced industrial countries. However, he explicitly coupled this "unity of action" with "merciless ideological struggle."

Crucially, Mandel denied that participating in united front action meant concluding that these parties were a "more progressive social class than the bourgeoisie." He identified those in power in countries like China and North Vietnam as representatives of the previous Communist parties and saw the ruling bureaucratic class as essentially recruited inside the Communist Party.

Matgamna acknowledges this complexity when he notes that "it was never uncritical adaptation — those who ceased to be critical ceased to be even nominally Trotskyist." Yet he immediately undermines this acknowledgment by reducing the FI's position to simple "adaptation." This is classic straw doll construction—acknowledging the complexity while simultaneously dismissing it.

The Nature of Post-Capitalist States: Dialectical Analysis vs. Mechanical Categories

Matgamna's critique fundamentally misrepresents Mandel's theoretical framework for understanding transitional societies. Rather than viewing countries like the USSR, China, and Cuba as examples of "socialism in one country," Mandel developed sophisticated analyses of what he termed "bureaucratically deformed" post-capitalist states.

Mandel's methodological approach criticized mechanical thinking incapable of handling categories of transition, combined and uneven development, and contradictory reality. He called for Marxists to embrace the sophisticated Marx rather than dogmatic simplifiers.

Mandel's framework acknowledged that the isolation of revolutions in backward countries led to forms of rule far from the classical Marxist ideal.

He viewed these as representing decisive steps toward self-emancipation and fundamental ruptures with the capitalist mode of production.

Crucially, Mandel never argued these societies had achieved socialism. He characterized transitional societies as having broken with capitalism but remaining marked by bureaucratic contradictions. He emphasized that the persistence of commodity production globally prevented the building of socialist society in isolated backward countries.

This nuanced theoretical framework, which recognized both the progressive character of the break with capitalism and the limitations imposed by isolation and bureaucracy, bears no resemblance to Matgamna's caricature of simple acceptance of "socialism in one country."

The "Double Struggle" Strategy

Mandel's response to the Australian SWP during the Soviet collapse reveals the sophistication of his strategic thinking. He argued that the working class and socialists in these states had to pursue a double struggle—against both capitalist restoration and bureaucratic rule.

This "double struggle" concept demonstrates the dialectical nature of Mandel's approach: recognizing that while these states were not capitalist, they were also not genuinely socialist. Workers needed to defend the gains of the revolution (nationalized property, planned economy) while fighting for genuine workers' democracy against bureaucratic usurpation.

This framework enabled Mandel to simultaneously oppose imperialist intervention while supporting movements like Solidarity in Poland, whose slogan "Give us back our factories!" represented precisely the kind of anti-bureaucratic political revolution that Trotskyist theory advocated.

The Historical Context: Permanent Revolution and Anti-Bureaucratic Struggle

The sources reveal that Mandel consistently defended the theory of permanent revolution against revisionist attacks from within the Trotskyist movement itself. When Jack Barnes of the American SWP argued in 1983 that permanent revolution was "an obstacle to reviving the tradition of Marx, Lenin and the first congresses of the Communist International," Mandel vigorously defended this core Trotskyist concept.

The Australian SWP went even further, calling permanent revolution a "useless fetish" and justifying "the Stalinist repression against Vietnamese Trotskyists." This historical context reveals that Mandel was defending orthodox Trotskyist positions against those who were actually abandoning them in favor of accommodation with Stalinist bureaucracies.

The "Mandelism" Label: Sectarian Rebranding

Matgamna's attempt to rebrand the Fourth International's politics as "Mandelism" rather than Trotskyism reveals the sectarian nature of his approach. He writes: "you, comrade Mandel, are the representative leader of post-Trotsky 'Trotskyism'. If it is to be given a special 'ism', then it must be 'Mandelism'."

This labeling serves a clear polemical function: by creating a false distinction between "real" Trotskyism and "post-Trotsky Trotskyism," Matgamna attempts to claim the mantle of orthodoxy while positioning himself as the guardian of pure doctrine. This is a classic sectarian maneuver that substitutes organizational and personal attacks for serious theoretical engagement.

The reality, documented throughout Mandel's work, is that he explicitly defended the continuity of revolutionary Marxism through Marx, Engels, Lenin, Trotsky, and the Fourth International. His theoretical work consistently advocated for building revolutionary organizations based on correct programs that respected internal democracy and the right of tendency.

Open Marxism vs. Schematic Dogmatism

Mandel's methodological approach reveals his commitment to developing Marxist theory that continually examines new evidence rather than relying on dogmatism. He maintained that Marxist theory must be scientific and capable of being tested against empirical reality.

This approach enabled Mandel to acknowledge theoretical errors and develop more sophisticated analyses when evidence demanded it. He developed his long wave theory through careful study of capitalism's actual development rather than mechanical repetition of formulas.

This intellectual honesty and theoretical development represents precisely the kind of living Marxist tradition that serious revolutionaries require, not the dogmatic approach that Matgamna's sectarian method represents.

The Ultimatum Strategy

Perhaps most revealing is Matgamna's ultimatum approach to political debate. He warns that if Trotskyists do not "face up to the facts, they will either drop out or take refuge in stark unreason: utterly defeated in the ideological struggle with the bourgeoisie, they will take refuge in fantasies and delusions."

This is not the language of comradely theoretical debate but of sectarian intimidation. Rather than engaging with the actual complexity of Mandel's theoretical contributions, Matgamna presents a binary choice: accept his interpretation or be condemned to "stark unreason."

This method serves the sectarian function that Mandel himself identified when confronting similar distortions: it serves to "homogenize and fanaticize" one's own membership by presenting easily dismissed alternatives rather than grappling with serious theoretical challenges.

The Stakes for Revolutionary Theory

The construction of straw dolls is not merely a tactical error—it represents a fundamental violation of the method necessary for advancing revolutionary theory. Marxism develops through honest confrontation with real challenges, not through demolishing invented positions.

Mandel's theoretical legacy—including his analysis of late capitalism, his framework for understanding transitional societies, and his strategic approach to revolutionary movements—represents decades of serious engagement with concrete historical developments. While this work certainly contains limitations and generates legitimate debates, it deserves engagement with its actual content rather than sectarian distortion.

The method Mandel consistently advocated—combining practical cooperation with "merciless ideological struggle"—provides a framework for principled engagement that could advance revolutionary theory through honest debate. Matgamna's approach, by contrast, forecloses such debate by substituting caricature for serious analysis.

Conclusion: The Pattern of Sectarian Distortion

Sean Matgamna's open letter reveals the bankruptcy of a method that substitutes caricature for serious engagement. By constructing straw dolls rather than addressing real positions, he forecloses the possibility of genuine theoretical advance.

The evidence from Mandel's extensive published works, contemporary debates, and responses to critics demonstrates that virtually every major claim in Matgamna's critique represents a distortion of Mandel's actual positions:

- **The "periphery fallacy"**: Mandel explicitly stated the decisive struggle was in capitalist centers, while supporting anti-imperialist struggles strategically

- **Crisis theory**: He developed sophisticated multicausal analysis grounded in Marx's method and extensive empirical study

- **"Adaptation"**: He advocated "unity of action alongside merciless ideological struggle," maintaining constant criticism of bureaucratic leaderships

- **Post-capitalist states**: He analyzed transitional societies with bureaucratic deformations, explicitly rejecting both "socialism in one country" and simple capitalist categories

- **Theoretical method**: He defended developing Marxist analysis against schematic dogmatism while maintaining core revolutionary principles

The historical context reveals that similar arguments were made by Ted Knight, Peter Taaffe, Jack Barnes, and the Australian SWP—all of whom later abandoned orthodox Trotskyist positions. This shows a pattern of sectarian critique that consistently distorts opponents' positions while claiming the mantle of orthodoxy.

Revolutionary Marxism deserves better than the distortions offered by the AWL's approach. The challenges facing the international working class demand theoretical tools capable of grappling with complex realities, not sectarian formulas that reduce everything to preconceived categories.

Ernest Mandel's legacy represents a serious attempt to develop Marxist analysis in response to concrete historical developments. The AWL's distortions serve only to obscure these contributions and impoverish revolutionary theory. The movement needs serious theoretical work that learns from both the achievements and limitations of revolutionary theory, not sectarian attacks that substitute denunciation for genuine analysis.

The task before serious Marxists is to restore honest debate based on actual positions, not invented caricatures. Only then can we hope to develop the theoretical tools necessary for the struggles ahead.

Internationalism and the Defense of Revolutionary Politics

Sean Matgamna's systematic distortion of Ernest Mandel's positions was never merely about settling theoretical accounts with a 'rival' who was barely aware of the AWL. By painting Mandel—the most prominent theorist of post-war Trotskyism—as an "adapter" who betrayed revolutionary principles, the AWL created the ideological space necessary to justify their own far more profound betrayals. Every false accusation hurled at Mandel served to normalise the AWL's accommodation to "democratic" capitalism: if authentic Trotskyism was "wrong" about everything, then supporting Yeltsin's restoration, Ireland's institutionalised sectarian division, and Zionist solutions could appear not as capitulation, but as theoretical progress. The slander was the method; social-democratic drift was the goal.

In this third installment of our response to Sean Matgamna's open letter to Ernest Mandel, we address one of the most fundamental questions in revolutionary theory: the relationship between world revolution and national isolation. Matgamna's letter attempts to characterize the Fourth International's theoretical development as an abandonment of internationalism in favor of adaptation to various "socialist" regimes. This represents not merely a misunderstanding of the FI's actual positions, but a complete inversion of the historical record that reveals the AWL's own trajectory away from revolutionary internationalism toward social-democratic accommodation.

The Fourth International's Unwavering Opposition to "Socialism in One Country"

The documentary evidence is unambiguous: Ernest Mandel and the Fourth International consistently and vehemently rejected Stalin's theory of "socialism in one country" throughout their entire political existence. The very foundation of the Fourth International in 1938 was a direct response to the perceived failures of social democracy and the rise of Stalinism, particularly Stalin's reactionary utopia of 'socialism in one country'.

As the "Declaration of the Four" (1933), a precursor to the FI's founding, made clear, the fundamental principles included recognition of the international and permanent character of the proletarian revolution and explicit rejection of the theory of socialism in a single country. The Fourth International's founding programme consistently emphasised that internationalism was inseparable from genuine socialism and that Stalin's abandonment of world revolution represented a fundamental betrayal of Marxist principles.

For Mandel and the FI, the theoretical foundation was crystal clear: the international character of the socialist revolution flows from the present state of economy and the social structure of humanity. Internationalism is no abstract principle but a theoretical and political reflection of the character of world economy, of the world development of productive forces and the world scale of the class struggle. The socialist revolution begins on national foundations — but it cannot be completed within these foundations.

The dissolution of the Comintern in 1943 was seen as Stalin putting the final point to his work of liquidation of the International, buried in 1934 under the auspices of 'socialism in one country'. This act broke the last formal link which united the USSR to the world proletarian revolution, by making national-socialism the official doctrine of the Soviet state.

Critical Solidarity vs. Sectarian Abstentionism

When Matgamna accuses the Fourth International of "adaptation" to various revolutionary movements, he fundamentally misrepresents the sophisticated methodology that Mandel developed for analyzing complex revolutionary processes. The FI's approach was not uncritical support, but rather what they termed "critical solidarity" - unconditional support for anti-imperialist struggles combined with consistent criticism of bureaucratic methods and advocacy for genuine workers' democracy.

Mandel's analysis, recognised at the Third World Congress in 1951, formally adopted this view that Stalinist communist parties could, under immense pressure from the masses in crisis situations, 'project a revolutionary orientation'. This was not an acceptance of "socialism on one country" as a desirable outcome, but an empirical observation that these parties, breaking from Moscow's direct control, could be driven to expropriate capitalism and establish "deformed workers' states."

Crucially, the FI maintained that the Yugoslav, Chinese, and Vietnamese communist parties came into direct conflict with Moscow to take power, and their victories were in no way the result of Moscow's policy. They characterised the Chinese Communist Party (CCP) as having a 'centrist-bureaucratic character' capable of leading a revolution but 'not a Stalinist party in the strict sense,' distinguishing it from the Kremlin's monolithic control.

This approach represents what Mandel called the "living tradition" of Marxism - the ability to analyze new phenomena concretely rather than dismissing them based on preconceived formulas. As Mandel wrote in a powerful passage defending dialectical analysis:

"Each one of us is against 'overinvestment', against 'gigantism', against Stalinist and post-Stalinist 'superindustrialisation', most of which represent a total loss of expenditure in material resources. But we are not against accelerated industrialisation as such in these countries or in Russia, which was the first to opt for it, after the October revolution. To turn one's back on this industrialisation would mean not just rejecting the whole short- and medium-term trend in economic policy elaborated by Lenin, Trotsky and the Left Opposition after 1923. Above all it would mean condemning those countries to flounder in barbarism while they wait for the victory of the world revolution. But when would that come about? After five years? After ten years? After 20 years? After 30 years? Who knows? Must we in the meantime fold our arms and tolerate the intolerable?"

This dialectical approach stood in sharp contrast to the sectarian abstentionism that characterizes much of the ultra-left, including the AWL's current positions on liberation struggles.

The AWL's Dangerous Support for Capitalist Restoration

While the Fourth International maintained its principled internationalism throughout the Cold War period, the AWL's trajectory during the collapse of the Soviet Union reveals how far they had drifted from revolutionary principles. The period 1989-1991 represents a watershed moment that exposes the AWL's fundamental abandonment of anti-capitalist politics in favor of abstract "democratic" principles.

The AWL will likely claim they supported 'democracy against totalitarianism' rather than capitalist restoration per se. But this defense only confirms our critique: their theoretical framework had evolved to a point where supporting bourgeois democracy against workers' states became not just acceptable, but principled. This represents precisely the kind of social-democratic drift that revolutionary Marxists must oppose.

During the August 1991 coup attempt, when hardline elements of the Soviet bureaucracy moved against Gorbachev, the AWL adopted a position of 'critical support' for Boris Yeltsin. As documented in their own theoretical evolution, the AWL had by this point abandoned the traditional Trotskyist analysis of the USSR as a 'degenerated workers' state' in favor of the formless

theory of treating the Soviet Union as a new form of class society with the bureaucracy as an exploiting class, similar to the theory 'bureaucratic collectivism' (but allowing the internal coexistence of a state-capitalist viewpoint).

This theoretical shift provided the justification for supporting capitalist restoration. If the USSR was indeed a new exploiting class society, then its overthrow, even by bourgeois forces, could be seen as a necessary step to dismantle totalitarianism and open up democratic space for future class struggle. The choice for AWL, informed by 'bureaucratic collectivism,' was to prioritise the overthrow of the workers' states as a prerequisite for any genuine workers' movement, even if the immediate outcome was capitalism.

The AWL may protest that they only gave 'critical support' to Yeltsin, not to capitalist restoration itself. But this misses the fundamental point: by 1991, their theoretical framework had evolved to make such 'critical support' not only possible but seemingly principled. When revolutionaries find themselves offering 'critical support' to figures implementing shock therapy and mass privatization, it is time to question the theoretical premises that led to such a position.

Yeltsin subsequently oversaw the implementation of neoliberal shock therapy, rapid privatisation, and the systematic destruction of the social gains of the October Revolution. As one analysis noted, this horrific product of mafia oligarchs working hand in hand with their imperialist patrons inflicted economic and social hardships so profound on the Russian people that, it is estimated, they were responsible for the deaths of at least three million people, along with a drop in the standard of living of the working class to a quarter of what it was in Soviet times.

A Pattern of Accommodation to Imperialism

The AWL's support for Yeltsin was not an isolated incident but part of a broader pattern of accommodation to "democratic" imperialism that continues to this day. Their trajectory demonstrates how the prioritization of abstract democratic principles over concrete class analysis leads inevitably to support for bourgeois solutions and ultimately imperialist interests.

On Ireland, the AWL has moved from early 'pioneering critiques of the Catholic-nationalist assumptions that had seeped into Irish left politics' to advocating for a 'federal united Ireland with regional autonomy for the mainly-Protestant north-east.' By 1998, the AWL's National Committee voted by a 'sizeable majority' for a 'yes' vote in the referendum on the Good Friday Agreement.

They acknowledged that the GFA 'erects institutions of power-sharing above the existing partition of Ireland' and 'tries to bury the basic question of two conflicting identities under a structure of balanced and weighted bureaucratic sectarianism.' Despite these criticisms and the GFA's entrenchment of partition, AWL considered it a 'lesser evil' if it 'holds and restrains armed communal conflict,' as it would 'create

easier conditions for working-class politics there.'

This represents a fundamental departure from the Fourth International's approach, which would view British rule in any part of Ireland as inherently illegitimate and prioritise a unified, independent Ireland achieved through revolutionary means rather than a negotiated settlement that entrenches partition through "power-sharing."

The AWL will likely defend their position by arguing that they were being 'realistic' about the existence of 'two communities' in Northern Ireland. But this 'realism' represents precisely the kind of accommodation to existing power structures that characterises social-democratic politics. Revolutionary organisations must certainly understand complex realities, but they cannot allow this understanding to lead them into supporting settlements that institutionalise imperialist partition.

Palestine: The Clearest Expression of AWL's Drift

On Palestine, the AWL's positions reveal most clearly their abandonment of anti-imperialist solidarity in favor of false 'evenhandedness' between oppressor and oppressed. The AWL adopted a 'two-state position on Israel-Palestine' in 1988 and advocates for 'two states and equal rights.'

More revealing still is their slogan 'No to Netanyahu, No to Hamas!' which creates a false equivalence between the forces of colonial oppression and those of anti-colonial resistance. This approach fundamentally abandons the principled internationalist position that would provide unequivocal solidarity with the Palestinian liberation struggle while maintaining criticism of particular tactical or strategic approaches.

The AWL may argue that their position is more 'nuanced' and takes account of the complexity of the situation. But revolutionary internationalism is not about appearing balanced or nuanced - it is about taking the side of the oppressed against their oppressors, regardless of the political character of the oppressed's current leadership.

The AWL's 'evenhandedness' between an imperialist state and a resistance movement reflects the same methodological error that led them to support Yeltsin: the subordination of class analysis to abstract democratic principles.

The Fourth International's current position on Palestine demonstrates the contrast: Building a global movement against genocide in Palestine demands unconditional solidarity with the oppressed against their oppressors, while maintaining the right to criticise particular leaderships or strategies.

The Method Behind the Deviation

The AWL's consistent pattern of deviation across multiple international questions reveals an underlying methodological problem: the subordination of concrete class analysis to abstract democratic principles.

This 'Third Camp' methodology, which emerged from their analysis of Stalinism as a totalitarian, anti-democratic regime, has led them to prioritize the fight against 'totalitarianism' and for 'democratic rights' over the fundamental class struggle for socialism.

As their program explicitly states, they are committed to 'democracy at every level of society, from the smallest workplace or community to global social organisation.' While this might sound progressive in abstract terms, in practice it leads to supporting bourgeois-democratic forces or outcomes, even when they entrench capitalism or imperialism, as seen in their stance on Yeltsin and the Good Friday Agreement.

The AWL's likely defense—that they are fighting for 'genuine democracy' rather than bourgeois democracy—only reveals the idealist character of their politics. They have developed an abstract concept of democracy divorced from its class content, allowing them to support 'democratic' solutions that serve imperialist interests while appearing to maintain revolutionary credentials.

This represents a fundamental departure from the Marxist understanding that views democracy not as an abstract principle but as a form of state power, ultimately serving the interests of the ruling class under capitalism.

For revolutionary Marxists, genuine democracy for the working class is achieved through class struggle, the overthrow of capitalism, and the establishment of workers' power based on workers' self-organization.

Internationalism vs. Social-Democratic Pragmatism

The contrast between the Fourth International's approach and that of the AWL illuminates two fundamentally different conceptions of internationalism. For the FI, internationalism means unwavering solidarity with all struggles against imperialism and exploitation, combined with principled criticism aimed at advancing the revolutionary potential of these movements.

For the AWL, 'internationalism' has been redefined to mean support for 'democratic' solutions that often align with imperialist interests when they come packaged in sufficiently liberal rhetoric. Their 'global solidarity against global capital' is filtered through a methodology that subordinates class struggle to abstract democratic principles.

This transformation represents precisely the kind of social-democratic drift that Trotsky warned against when founding the Fourth International. The accommodation to "realistic" solutions, the prioritisation of parliamentary democracy over workers' power, and the abandonment of revolutionary internationalism in favour of pragmatic reformism - all of these characteristics mark the AWL's evolution away from revolutionary Marxism.

Contemporary Relevance

The theoretical and political questions raised by the AWL's trajectory have profound contemporary relevance. In an era marked by renewed inter-imperialist conflict, rising movements for national liberation, and deepening capitalist crisis, the choice between revolutionary internationalism and social-democratic accommodation has never been more stark.

The AWL's method leads consistently to supporting the 'lesser evil' of bourgeois democracy against more authoritarian forms of capitalism, even when this means accommodating imperialism. This approach renders revolutionary organisations incapable of providing principled leadership to the struggles that will define the coming period.

The Fourth International's approach, by contrast, maintains the possibility of revolutionary transformation precisely because it refuses to subordinate class struggle to the false choices imposed by bourgeois politics. By maintaining principled solidarity with all anti-imperialist struggles while advocating for genuine workers' democracy, the FI preserves the revolutionary potential that the AWL has systematically abandoned.

Conclusion: The Living Tradition vs. Sectarian Adaptation

Sean Matgamna's accusation that the Fourth International "adapted" to various revolutionary movements represents a complete inversion of the actual historical record. It was the AWL that adapted - not to revolutionary movements, but to bourgeois-democratic imperialism dressed up in the language of human rights and democracy.

The AWL may protest that this characterisation is unfair, that they maintain their commitment to socialism and workers' power. But political organisations must be judged by their concrete positions on key international questions, not by their abstract commitments. When an organisation consistently finds itself supporting 'democratic' solutions that align with imperialist interests—from Yeltsin's Russia to partitioned Ireland to a two-state solution in Palestine—the pattern reveals more than the sum of its parts.

The Fourth International's theoretical development under Mandel's leadership represented the "living tradition" of Marxism in action: the ability to analyze new phenomena concretely while maintaining fidelity to fundamental revolutionary principles. This approach allowed them to support anti-imperialist struggles without illusions about their leaderships, to defend the gains of post-capitalist societies while criticizing their bureaucratic deformations, and to maintain revolutionary internationalism while adapting tactics to changing conditions.

The AWL's trajectory, by contrast, shows how the abandonment of dialectical analysis in favor of abstract principles leads inevitably toward accommodation with the existing order. Their 'orthodoxy' became a rigid schema that could only be maintained by systematically distorting the positions of more sophisticated revolutionaries.

Some may argue that this critique is too harsh, that the AWL simply made errors in judgment while maintaining their revolutionary intent. But the consistency of their deviations across multiple international questions suggests something deeper than tactical mistakes. When theoretical errors lead systematically to positions that accommodate imperialism and capitalism, they cease to be merely errors and become a pattern that demands explanation.

In our next article, we will examine how this methodological problem manifests in the AWL's approach to democratic questions, showing how their retreat from revolutionary solutions in Ireland and Palestine represents part of a broader idealist deviation that prioritizes bourgeois-democratic forms over the material interests of the working class.

The choice facing revolutionary socialists today remains the same as it was when Trotsky founded the Fourth International: between the living tradition of revolutionary Marxism and the various forms of accommodation to the existing order. The AWL's trajectory serves as a warning of how even organizations that claim revolutionary credentials can drift toward social-democratic pragmatism when they abandon the concrete analysis of concrete conditions in favor of abstract principles divorced from class struggle.

Critics may argue that this analysis is sectarian, that it fails to acknowledge the genuine difficulties facing revolutionary organizations in complex political situations. But there is nothing sectarian about insisting that revolutionary organizations maintain revolutionary positions. The 'complexity' that leads to supporting Yeltsin, the Good Friday

Agreement, and two-state solutions is not the complexity of revolutionary dialectics—it is the complexity of trying to maintain socialist rhetoric while accommodating capitalist reality.

Ernest Mandel's legacy stands as a beacon for all those committed to the difficult but necessary work of developing revolutionary theory for contemporary conditions while maintaining unwavering solidarity with all those who struggle against imperialism and exploitation.

Postscript: On the AWL's Irish "Solution"

It would be easy to characterise the AWL's federal Irish solution as mere repartition, since it would leave the internal arrangements within Ulster largely unchanged—the same sectarian institutions, the same communal divisions, the same Protestant autonomy that partition originally created. However, it is more accurate to describe their approach as "institutionalised sectarian division" since defence and foreign policy would formally pass to Dublin, creating a single Irish state albeit one internally divided along communal lines.

This transition might indeed prove smoother than critics initially assumed. The Good Friday Agreement has already given Ireland decades of experience in oversight and consultation regarding Northern Ireland. While the GFA doesn't grant the Irish government direct executive authority over Northern Ireland's defence or foreign policy, it established formal structures and frameworks for consultation, cooperation, and input on issues concerning Northern Ireland. The AWL's federal proposal would simply formalise what has been evolving through practice—Irish involvement in Northern affairs, but within structures that permanently entrench the sectarian divisions that British imperialism originally imposed.

The fundamental critique remains: rather than challenging the legacy of divide-and-rule, the AWL's approach constitutionally enshrines it. This represents accommodation to imperialism's most enduring achievement—the successful division of the Irish working class along religious and national lines.

The Collapse of the USSR: Vindication, Not Refutation

Sean Matgamna's central accusation against Ernest Mandel could not be more direct: "The collapse of the USSR shows conclusively that your version of 'Trotskyism' was radically wrong, false, and disorienting." This represents the Alliance for Workers' Liberty's strongest argument—their supposed ace in the hole that allegedly demolishes not just Mandel's analysis, but the entire theoretical framework of the Fourth International.

Yet a careful examination of the historical record reveals something far more devastating for the AWL: the collapse of the USSR represents one of the most spectacular vindications of Mandel's theoretical framework in the history of Marxist analysis. Far from being "radically wrong," Mandel's predictions about the USSR's trajectory proved remarkably prescient, while alternative theories—including those favored by the AWL—failed to account for the specific dynamics of how and why the Soviet system collapsed.

The AWL's Theoretical Incoherence: State Capitalism or Bureaucratic Collectivism?

The AWL's defense will be complicated by their own internal theoretical incoherence. After decades of debate, they have never formally resolved whether the USSR was "state capitalist" (following some version of Tony Cliff's analysis) or represented "bureaucratic collectivism" (a new exploiting class). This theoretical confusion is revealing: both currents within the AWL supported Yeltsin's rise to power despite their different analyses of what the USSR actually was.

As Martin Thomas acknowledged in his critique of state capitalist theory, Cliff's framework faces the fundamental problem that "a capital which no longer competes with other capitals is not a capital in the Marxian sense." Thomas noted that state capitalist theories could only be defended "by reasoning with dubious analogies" and concluded that "not a single theory of state capitalism succeeded in being both orthodox-Marxist as well as consistent with the facts."

Similarly, Paul Hampton's assessment of bureaucratic collectivism noted that such theories "cannot pretend consistency with Marxian orthodoxy" and face the problem that they describe "a ruling class [that] emerged which did not exist as a class before it came to power." Both theoretical positions led to the same political conclusion: supporting what they characterized as the progressive overthrow of a totalitarian system.

For the AWL's state capitalist wing, if the USSR was already capitalist, their entire narrative of "capitalist restoration" becomes theoretically incoherent. For their bureaucratic collectivist wing, the collapse meant the overthrow of a "new exploiting class"—but this still led them to welcome bourgeois democracy as progress.

The Prophetic Framework: Mandel's "Transitional Society" Analysis

Mandel's analysis was fundamentally different from both AWL variants.

He characterized the USSR as a "transitional society"—neither fully socialist nor capitalist, but a unique social formation emerging from the October Revolution's abolition of private property, yet deformed by parasitic bureaucratic rule.

Crucially, Mandel argued this was not a stable formation but one marked by constant pressure toward resolution—either through political revolution by the working class or capitalist restoration by the bureaucracy. This framework allowed him to make specific predictions about the dynamics of collapse that proved remarkably accurate.

The Documented Predictions: Mandel's Warnings About Capitalist Restoration

The documentary evidence demolishes the AWL's claim that Mandel was caught off-guard by the USSR's collapse. The project materials show that Mandel explicitly warned about the possibility of capitalist restoration and predicted the specific form it would take.

Mandel's analysis identified the structural contradictions that would drive the system toward crisis and the mechanisms by which restoration would occur. His framework predicted both the system's instability and the violent, chaotic character restoration would assume—predictions that proved tragically accurate.

The AWL's Documented Support for Yeltsin's Rise

Martin Thomas's own survey of Trotskyist responses to the August 1991 events documents the AWL's position clearly. As Socialist Organiser, they issued materials opposing the coup and supporting what they explicitly characterized as a "bourgeois revolution."

Thomas, co-leader of the AWL current for much of the last 50 years, with quotes Socialist Organiser's assessment: "What we are witnessing in the USSR is a bourgeois revolution. The leaders of the anti-Stalinist revolution and their ideas; the ideas in the heads of the mass of the people (including the working class); the West European and US social models they look to - all define it as a bourgeois revolution."

This wasn't accidental—it flowed directly from their theoretical analysis. Whether viewing the USSR as state capitalist or bureaucratic collectivist, both currents within the AWL had concluded that the system represented a form of exploitation that needed to be overthrown, even if the immediate outcome was capitalism.

The "Double Struggle" Strategy: Against Both Bureaucracy and Restoration

The AWL's critique reduces Mandel's position to simple "defense of Stalinism." This represents a fundamental distortion. The project materials show that Mandel consistently advocated what he termed a "double struggle"—defending the gains of the October Revolution while simultaneously fighting the bureaucracy that had usurped workers' power.

This strategy was evident in Mandel's support for anti-bureaucratic movements throughout Eastern Europe, including the Polish Solidarity movement. The "double struggle" framework enabled Mandel to simultaneously oppose imperialist intervention while supporting workers' movements against bureaucratic rule.

Post-Collapse Vindication: The Nature of Russian "Mafia Capitalism"

The specific form that capitalist restoration took provides powerful vindication of Mandel's analysis. The emergence of Russian oligarchy—where former nomenklatura members transformed themselves into private proprietors—matched what Mandel had predicted about the bureaucracy's drive to secure privileges through private property ownership.

The "shock therapy" of the 1990s, with its massive economic contraction and social devastation, confirmed Mandel's warnings about the violent character restoration would assume. As one analysis notes, this process was "responsible for the deaths of at least three million people, along with a drop in the standard of living of the working class to a quarter of what it was in Soviet times."

The Failure of Alternative Theories

While Mandel's framework provided accurate predictions, the AWL's alternative theories struggled to explain what actually happened. Both state capitalist and bureaucratic collectivist theories faced fundamental problems in accounting for the specific dynamics of collapse and restoration.

State capitalist theories faced the logical problem of explaining "restoration" if capitalism already existed. Bureaucratic collectivist theories struggled to explain why their supposed "new ruling class" would dismantle its own distinct form of exploitation rather than defending it.

The False Binary of "Democracy vs. Totalitarianism"

The AWL will likely defend their support for Yeltsin by claiming they were fighting for "democracy against totalitarianism." This defense only confirms our critique: their theoretical framework had evolved to a point where supporting bourgeois democracy against degenerated workers' states became not just acceptable, but principled.

Their critique of Mandel served to justify their own accommodation to "democratic" capitalism: if authentic Trotskyism was "wrong" about everything, then supporting capitalist restoration could appear not as capitulation, but as theoretical progress.

The Pattern of Accommodation: A Broader Trajectory

The AWL's support for Yeltsin was not isolated but part of a broader pattern of accommodation to "democratic" imperialism. Their positions on

Ireland (supporting the Good Friday Agreement despite acknowledging it "erects institutions of power-sharing above the existing partition") and Palestine (their "No to Netanyahu, No to Hamas!" slogan creating false equivalence between oppressor and oppressed) reflect the same methodological errors.

Open Marxism vs. Sectarian Dogmatism

The fundamental issue is method itself. Mandel's approach represented dialectical analysis that could develop in response to concrete conditions while maintaining revolutionary principles. As he wrote in <u>defending this approach</u>:

"Each one of us is against 'overinvestment', against 'gigantism', against Stalinist and post-Stalinist 'superindustrialisation', most of which represent a total loss of expenditure in material resources. But we are not against accelerated industrialisation as such in these countries or in Russia, which was the first to opt for it, after the October revolution... Above all it would mean condemning those countries to flounder in barbarism while they wait for the victory of the world revolution. But when would that come about? After five years? After ten years? After 20 years? After 30 years? Who knows? Must we in the meantime fold our arms and tolerate the intolerable?"

The AWL's method, by contrast, subordinates concrete analysis to predetermined schemas, rendering them incapable of understanding complex historical developments.

Conclusion

The collapse of the USSR represents not the refutation of Mandel's analysis but its vindication. His characterization of the Soviet system as an unstable transitional society, his warnings about capitalist restoration, and his predictions about the violent character restoration would assume all proved accurate.

The AWL's critique reveals the poverty of their own method. Their claim that the collapse proved Mandel wrong rests on fundamental misrepresentations of what he actually predicted. More damaging, their mechanical approach—reducing everything to predetermined categories—rendered them incapable of analyzing concrete political developments.

The choice facing revolutionary Marxists today is between Mandel's living tradition—theory that develops through engagement with concrete struggles while maintaining revolutionary principles—and the AWL's sectarian method that subordinates reality to predetermined schemas. The collapse of the USSR provides a definitive test of these approaches, and history has rendered its verdict: Mandel's framework proved far superior to the alternatives promoted by his critics.

The Chinese Revolution and Contemporary Strategy

From Historical Vindication to Contemporary Strategy

Sean Matgamna's most detailed theoretical challenge to Ernest Mandel centers on the Chinese Revolution.

He asks pointedly: "Do you agree that a peasant army headed by a peasant party and with a petty-bourgeois Stalinist leadership destroyed capitalist property and peasant farms leading to the dictatorship of the proletariat without a new revolution?"

He frames this as exposing a fundamental flaw—that Mandel's analysis implies "a peaceful, gradual transition from a bourgeois state to a workers' state," representing a "reformist scenario" that abandons Marxist theory.

This critique appears substantial because it touches on core questions of revolutionary strategy: the role of the peasantry, the nature of state power, and the dynamics of permanent revolution.

Yet a careful examination reveals that Matgamna's challenge rests on the same systematic misrepresentation that characterizes his entire approach.

More significantly, the debate over China illuminates contemporary questions about how revolutionary organizations should relate to movements that don't emerge from "pure" proletarian leadership—questions that have become urgent in an era of climate crisis, anti-racist upheaval, and global resistance to imperialism.

The China Question: Mandel's Sophisticated Analysis vs. AWL Caricature

To understand why Matgamna's critique fails, we must examine what Mandel actually argued about the Chinese Revolution rather than the straw doll Matgamna constructs. The Alliance for Workers' Liberty presents Mandel as endorsing "peasant socialism" and abandoning the revolutionary role of the proletariat. The documentary record tells a dramatically different story.

Mandel's Framework: Permanent Revolution Confirmed, Not Abandoned

Far from viewing the Chinese Revolution as a "peaceful, gradual transition," Mandel consistently argued that it confirmed Trotsky's theory of permanent revolution.

In his debate with Doug Jenness, Mandel was explicit: "In Russia, Yugoslavia, China, Vietnam, Cuba and Nicaragua it was necessary to destroy the bourgeoisie's state and army, and the state of the dictatorship of the proletariat had to be created in order to carry out the national-democratic tasks of the revolution. The strategy of permanent revolution was confirmed 100 per cent in all these revolutions."

This demolishes Matgamna's central claim. Mandel didn't argue for gradual transition: he insisted that revolutionary transformation required the violent destruction of the bourgeois state apparatus and its replacement with proletarian power.

The Chinese Revolution represented not an exception to permanent revolution but its confirmation under specific historical conditions.

The Peasantry Question: Dialectical Analysis vs. Mechanical Formulas

Matgamna's challenge about the "peasant army" reveals his mechanical understanding of class dynamics. He treats Mandel's analysis as if it placed the peasantry in an independent revolutionary role, contradicting Marxist theory about class leadership in revolution.

But Mandel's actual position followed Trotsky's analysis precisely: "the peasantry cannot form a truly independent political force from the bourgeoisie or proletariat."

The peasantry is "historically compelled to align with either the bourgeoisie or the proletariat, and a victorious revolution necessitates the 'hegemony of the proletariat.'"

The Chinese Revolution succeeded not because peasants acted independently, but because the Communist Party, despite its bureaucratic deformations, ultimately aligned with proletarian rather than bourgeois interests in the context of anti-imperialist struggle.

As Mandel noted, the Chinese Communist Party "had to come into direct conflict with Moscow in order to take power," and its victory represented "overthrowing capitalism" rather than accommodation with it.

The "Stalinist Leadership" Question: Critical Support vs. Uncritical Adaptation

Matgamna's reference to "petty-bourgeois Stalinist leadership" attempts to trap Mandel in apparent contradiction: how can a Trotskyist support a revolution led by Stalinists?

This challenge would be devastating if Mandel had indeed offered uncritical support to Mao's regime. But the evidence shows the opposite.

The Fourth International's position combined "unconditional support to the struggle for the defense of the Chinese revolution against imperialism" with explicit criticism of the CCP's bureaucratic methods.

Mandel characterized the Chinese revolution as a "bureaucratic caricature, carried out from the top by the Stalinist bureaucracy," while insisting that it nonetheless represented a genuine overthrow of capitalism.

This approach, supporting the anti-imperialist content while criticizing the bureaucratic form, exemplifies precisely the kind of dialectical analysis that Matgamna's mechanical framework cannot accommodate.

The Fourth International didn't choose between pure support or pure opposition; it developed a nuanced position that could distinguish between the progressive content of anti-capitalist transformation and the limitations of its bureaucratic leadership.

The Cultural Revolution: Mandel's Critical Analysis

Mandel's analysis of the Cultural Revolution further demolishes any suggestion that he uncritically supported Maoist policies. He characterized it as "the most complex phenomenon faced by revolutionary Marxists in recent decades," viewing it as essentially "a conflict within the bureaucracy where contending factions appealed to the masses" rather than genuine democratization.

Mandel criticized Mao's "abandonment of Marxist sociology by attributing the danger of degeneration to ideological factors rather than the material infrastructure of society." He noted the "general absence of genuine workers' councils or soviet-type organs in Chinese industrial plants" and condemned the "systematic organization of the 'Mao cult'" as serving "inter-bureaucratic power struggles rather than genuine democracy."

This represents exactly the kind of "merciless ideological struggle" that Mandel advocated: maintaining support for the revolution's gains while providing sharp criticism of its bureaucratic limitations. Such an approach required theoretical sophistication that the AWL's black-and-white framework simply cannot provide.

Historical Vindication: How Events Proved Mandel's Framework Correct

The subsequent history of China provides powerful vindication of Mandel's theoretical framework, though not in the way his critics might expect. His analysis of China as a "deformed workers' state" proved accurate precisely because it predicted the possibility of capitalist restoration if political revolution failed to emerge. Like the USSR, China became trapped in a transitional phase that, without genuine workers' democracy, inevitably moved toward capitalist restoration.

The Market Reforms: Inevitable Bureaucratic Trajectory

When China began market reforms in the 1980s, this confirmed rather than refuted Mandel's analysis. The specific form these reforms took—with Communist Party members becoming the new capitalist class while maintaining political control—matches exactly what Mandel had predicted about bureaucratic self-interest driving toward private property ownership.

Mandel had warned that "the bureaucracy's pressure to obtain permanent ties with specific factories or enterprises... all point towards the potential emergence of a 'good old capitalist one, based upon private property.'" The emergence of "red capitalists" and the transformation of party cadres into business owners represents precisely this dynamic.

Contemporary China: From Deformed Workers' State to Capitalist Restoration

While Ernest Mandel's framework of a "deformed workers' state" provided a nuanced analysis of China's post-revolutionary trajectory, subsequent developments have demonstrably led to a full rollback to capitalism and the emergence of China as a major imperialist power. Like the USSR, China became stuck in the transitional phase, and only a political revolution could have prevented capitalist restoration.

The evidence is now overwhelming that China's dominant mode of production is unequivocally capitalist. As Pierre Rousset notes, China is "at the heart of the world capitalist system" and "in the Chinese CP you have billionaires," indicating a complete departure from proletarian principles. Ana Cristina Carvalhaes emphasizes that "what rules in China is the law of value" despite state direction, describing it as a "very lively capitalism."

This capitalist restoration was not merely an unintended consequence but, in the absence of a renewed political revolution, an almost inevitable outcome that Mandel himself had foreseen. He had warned of the bureaucracy's "pressure to obtain permanent ties with specific factories or enterprises... all point towards the potential emergence of a 'good old capitalist one, based upon private property.'" The transformation of party cadres into business owners and the rise of "red capitalists" exemplify this dynamic perfectly.

Furthermore, China has cemented its position as what Pierre Rousset identifies as "a new imperialist power," becoming "the second largest imperialist power in the world on economic terms." Its "expansionist policy," including militarization in the China Sea and the Belt and Road Initiative, are clear characteristics of imperialism.

From China to Contemporary Strategy: The Relevance of Mandel's Method

The debate over the Chinese Revolution illuminates fundamental questions facing revolutionary organizations today, made more urgent by the trajectory China has actually followed. China's development from a deformed workers' state to a major capitalist imperialist power demonstrates both the accuracy of Mandel's theoretical framework and the tragic consequences when political revolution fails to develop. How should revolutionaries relate to movements that emerge under non-proletarian leadership? What attitude should they take toward struggles that achieve progressive goals through problematic means? How can organizations maintain revolutionary principles while engaging with actually existing social movements? China's trajectory toward capitalist restoration makes these questions more urgent, not less relevant.

The Climate Movement: Applying Mandel's Framework

Consider the contemporary climate movement. Much of it emerges under liberal or even bourgeois leadership, often advocating market-based solutions rather than systemic transformation. Applying the AWL's logic to climate organizing would require rejecting any movement not led by the organized working class or not explicitly anti-capitalist.

Mandel's approach provides a superior framework: unconditional support for struggles against fossil fuel extraction while maintaining "merciless ideological struggle" against inadequate leadership and limited solutions. This allows revolutionary organizations to engage with actually existing movements while pushing for more radical approaches—exactly the kind of dialectical engagement that effective revolutionary strategy requires.

BDS and Palestine Solidarity: The Contemporary China Question

The Boycott, Divestment, and Sanctions movement provides another illuminating parallel. BDS emerged under Palestinian nationalist rather than explicitly socialist leadership, includes liberal and even some conservative participants, and focuses on specific reforms rather than revolutionary transformation. The AWL's mechanical approach leads them to support "two-state solutions" precisely because they cannot engage dialectically with movements that don't fit predetermined schemas.

Mandel's framework would suggest unconditional support for Palestinian resistance to colonialism while maintaining criticism of nationalist limitations and advocating for revolutionary solutions. The experience of China—and indeed Cuba, which currently faces a "crossroads" and the danger of evolving toward a "Chinese-Vietnamese type system" without political reforms—reinforces the critical importance of sustained revolutionary po-

litical processes. Economic transformation alone, without genuine workers' democracy, proves insufficient to prevent capitalist restoration. This makes the questions of revolutionary strategy in the contemporary period even more pressing.

Anti-Racist Movements: Beyond Purity Politics

Contemporary anti-racist movements often emerge under liberal leadership, focus on reform rather than revolution, and include significant middle-class participation. The AWL's approach tends toward either sectarian abstention from such movements or complete adaptation to their liberal politics.

Mandel's method provides a third way: active participation in struggles against racist oppression combined with advocacy for revolutionary approaches that link anti-racism to anti-capitalism. This requires the kind of theoretical sophistication that can distinguish between the progressive content of anti-racist struggle and the limitations of its current leadership—precisely what Mandel demonstrated in analyzing China.

The Fourth International's Contemporary Strategy: Useful Anti-Capitalist Parties

The Fourth International's evolution toward building useful anti-capitalist parties represents the practical application of lessons learned from analyzing movements like the Chinese Revolution. Rather than waiting for pure revolutionary conditions or maintaining sectarian isolation, the FI advocates building formations that can unite diverse anti-capitalist forces while maintaining revolutionary perspectives.

The "New Period, New Programme, New Party" Framework

The Fourth International's strategic evolution recognizes that effective revolutionary organizations must be capable of relating to movements as they actually exist rather than as revolutionaries wish they existed. This means building parties that can include "currents of various origins: Trotskyists of different kinds, libertarians, revolutionary syndicalists, revolutionary nationalists, left reformists."

This approach applies Mandel's China analysis to contemporary organizational questions: how can revolutionaries maintain principled positions while engaging with forces that don't start from pure revolutionary premises? The answer requires exactly the kind of dialectical thinking that Mandel brought to analyzing the Chinese Revolution.

Contemporary Examples: Learning from Success and Failure

The Fourth International's involvement in building formations like PSOL in Brazil, Sinistra Critica in Italy, and the New Anti-Capitalist Party in France represents attempts to apply these lessons practically. These experiences, with their successes and limitations, provide concrete examples of how revolutionary organizations can

engage with broader anti-capitalist currents while maintaining revolutionary identity.

The key insight from Mandel's China analysis applies directly: the content of these formations matters more than their formal leadership structure. A party that maintains anti-capitalist positions and democratic internal life while including diverse tendencies represents progress over sectarian isolation, even if its leadership includes non-revolutionary elements.

The AWL's Contemporary Irrelevance: Where Sectarian Purity Leads

The Alliance for Workers' Liberty's inability to engage dialectically with complex movements has rendered them largely irrelevant to contemporary struggles. Their mechanical framework prevents them from relating effectively to climate movements, anti-racist organizing, Palestine solidarity, or other vital contemporary struggles.

The Pattern of Accommodation to Imperialism

When forced to choose between sectarian purity and practical engagement, the AWL consistently chooses accommodation to "democratic" imperialism over solidarity with liberation struggles. Their support for two-state solutions in Palestine, acceptance of the Good Friday Agreement in Ireland, and various other positions reflect this pattern.

This represents the practical consequence of their theoretical method:

unable to engage dialectically with complex movements, they retreat to supporting "realistic" solutions that often align with imperialist interests. Their critique of Mandel's China analysis serves to justify this broader trajectory of accommodation.

The Climate Crisis and Revolutionary Strategy

The urgency of climate crisis makes the AWL's sectarian approach particularly destructive. Effective climate organizing requires precisely the kind of broad anti-capitalist unity that Mandel's method enables. Organizations that demand pure revolutionary leadership before engaging with climate struggles will remain marginal while the planet burns.

The choice facing the left is between Mandel's approach—principled engagement with actually existing movements combined with advocacy for revolutionary solutions—and the AWL's method, which leads either to sectarian isolation or opportunist accommodation to bourgeois politics.

Lessons for 21st Century Revolutionary Strategy

The debate over the Chinese Revolution illuminates fundamental questions about revolutionary strategy that have become urgent in the contemporary period. The choice is not between the AWL's "realism" and alleged "romantic" support for any movement that claims to be revolutionary. It is between two fundamentally different approaches to revolutionary politics.

Again, For Living, Open Marxism vs. Sectarian Schemas

Mandel's approach to China exemplifies what he called "living Marxism" and "open Marxism": theory that develops through engagement with concrete struggles rather than mechanical application of predetermined formulas. This approach enabled accurate analysis of complex phenomena like the Chinese Revolution while maintaining revolutionary principles (and which rejected mechanical determinism).

The AWL's approach represents the opposite: mechanical application of abstract schemas that cannot accommodate the complexity of actually existing struggles. This method leads either to sectarian irrelevance or opportunist adaptation, as their contemporary positions demonstrate.

Building Revolutionary Organizations for the Climate Crisis Era

The contemporary period demands revolutionary organizations capable of relating to movements that emerge under diverse leadership while maintaining anti-capitalist perspectives. The climate crisis, rising fascism, and global resistance to imperialism create conditions that require exactly the kind of broad anti-capitalist unity that Mandel's approach enables.

Revolutionary organizations that demand ideological purity before engaging with mass movements will remain irrelevant to the struggles that will define the coming period. Those that can combine principled positions with tactical flexibility, following Mandel's model of "unity of action with merciless ideological struggle," have the potential to provide revolutionary leadership to these movements.

The Stakes of Theoretical Method

The debate over Ernest Mandel's analysis of the Chinese Revolution is not merely historical. It illuminates the choice between theoretical approaches that can advance revolutionary strategy in the 21st century and those that render revolutionary organizations incapable of relating to actually existing struggles.

Matgamna's critique of Mandel represents more than disagreement over historical events—it reflects a broader methodological approach that has led the AWL toward accommodation with imperialism and irrelevance to contemporary movements. Their inability to understand how Mandel could simultaneously support the Chinese Revolution and maintain revolutionary principles reveals the poverty of their own theoretical framework.

Conclusion: Revolutionary Strategy for a New Era

The Alliance for Workers' Liberty's critique of Ernest Mandel's analysis of the Chinese Revolution represents their strongest remaining substantive argument. Yet examination of the historical record reveals that this critique, like their others, rests on systematic misrepresentation of Mandel's actual positions combined with mechanical application of abstract schemas to complex historical phenomena.

Mandel's analysis of China as a "deformed workers' state" provided a framework that proved remarkably accurate in predicting the trajectory toward capitalist restoration that China has indeed followed. His warning that transitional societies would move toward either workers' democracy or capitalist restoration was tragically confirmed when political revolution failed to develop and China became a major imperialist power. His approach of combining unconditional support for anti-imperialist struggle with "merciless ideological struggle" against bureaucratic limitations exemplifies the kind of dialectical analysis that effective revolutionary strategy requires.

More importantly, the debate over China illuminates fundamental questions facing revolutionary organizations in the contemporary period. The climate crisis, rising fascism, and global resistance to imperialism create conditions that demand exactly the kind of broad anti-capitalist unity that Mandel's approach enables. Revolutionary organizations must be capable of relating to movements as they actually exist while maintaining revolutionary perspectives, precisely what Mandel demonstrated in analyzing the Chinese Revolution.

The Fourth International's evolution toward building useful anti-capitalist parties represents the practical application of these insights to contemporary conditions. Rather than demanding ideological purity before engaging with mass movements, this approach seeks to build formations that can unite diverse anti-capitalist forces while maintaining revolutionary identity.

The AWL's trajectory demonstrates the alternative: mechanical application of abstract schemas leads either to sectarian irrelevance or opportunist accommodation to bourgeois politics. Their critique of Mandel serves to justify a broader pattern of accommodation to "democratic" imperialism that renders them incapable of providing revolutionary leadership to contemporary struggles.

The choice facing revolutionary socialists in the 21st century is between these approaches: living, open Marxism that develops through engagement with concrete struggles, or sectarian dogmatism that substitutes abstract principles for dialectical analysis. Ernest Mandel's legacy provides essential tools for building the kind of revolutionary organizations capable of responding to contemporary crises while maintaining unwavering commitment to human emancipation.

The stakes could not be higher. The climate crisis demands urgent action that transcends traditional organizational boundaries. Rising fascism requires united resistance that cannot afford sectarian divisions. Global resistance to imperialism needs solidarity that goes beyond narrow ideological conformity. Mandel's approach—principled engagement with actually existing movements combined with advocacy for revolutionary solutions—provides a framework for building the broad anti-capitalist unity that these struggles demand.

The Alliance for Workers' Liberty's critique of Mandel's China analysis reveals not the poverty of his approach but the sterility of their own. Their inability to understand how revolutionaries can simultaneously support liberation struggles and maintain revolutionary principles reflects a broader theoretical rigidity that has rendered them irrelevant to the movements that will define the coming period.

Those committed to building effective revolutionary organizations for the 21st century would do well to study how Mandel's method enabled sophisticated analysis of complex revolutionary processes while maintaining fundamental revolutionary principles. The alternative—the AWL's path toward sectarian irrelevance or opportunist accommodation—offers nothing to the struggles against climate catastrophe, fascist reaction, and imperialist oppression that will determine humanity's future.

Part Three

How Sectarian Dishonesty Distorts Revolutionary History

The 1953 East Berlin Uprising and the Fourth International

The disagreement over whether the Fourth International's International Secretariat called for Soviet troop withdrawal during the 1953 East Berlin uprising reveals something important about how organized Trotskyist tendencies conduct polemic. The Lambert current's claim (repeated by the AWL's open letter) that the world Trotskyist movement refused this demand is not merely wrong; it's dishonest in a specific, instructive way.[1]

It misrepresents what the IS actually said to delegitimize an opponent rather than engaging the real political differences. This matters because left organizations regularly deploy this tactic. Understanding how it works makes you a better organizer and a more discerning reader of left organizational critique.

The Accusation: A Clean, Devastating Narrative

The conventional Lambertist narrative carries rhetorical force. According to this version, Pablo and the International Secretariat capitulated to Stalinism by refusing to demand Soviet withdrawal during the Berlin uprising. They called for "the real democratisation of the Communist Parties," effectively seeking to reform rather than overthrow the bureaucracy. By avoiding explicit demands that Russian tanks

leave, they revealed their accommodation to Soviet interests. This wasn't disagreement over strategy; it was betrayal of revolutionary principle.

If true, this accusation would confirm everything the Lambertists claimed about Pabloite revisionism. It would show that when workers actually rebelled against the Stalinist apparatus, the IS leadership abandoned revolutionary intransigence precisely when it mattered most. The evidence would be damning: a formal declaration, a written record, proof of capitulation in the moment of crisis.

The narrative is compelling. It's also false.

What the IS Actually Said

The International Secretariat's declaration on the 1953 uprising, issued on June 25, hailed the workers' revolt as the "first salvo of the political revolution in the East." The analysis, informed by reports from IS members active in Berlin and East Germany, characterized the events as a revolutionary movement of the working class against the bureaucratic and police political regime. The IS endorsed the striking workers' demands and called for the restoration of freely elected workers' councils.

---

[1] Sean Matgamna's mistaken claim, that the Fourth International did not oppose the withdrawal of Soviet troops at the time of the 1953 uprising in East Berlin, most likely originated in the OCI, Pierre Lambert's organization. It was the French sister of the Socialist

Labour League in Britain, which Matgamna was a member of until 1963. Months after completing the five preceding articles in this series, we found that in the 1960s and as late as 1970 Lambert's OCI had made this claim.

Here is the critical part that Lambertist polemic systematically omits: The International also reiterated its standing call for the withdrawal of all occupation troops from Germany. All of them. Soviet, American, British, and French.

Not just Soviet troops. Not with ambiguity. Not hedged or conditional. All occupying forces.

This was an internationalist demand. It refused the bloc politics that characterized Cold War thinking. It said: workers cannot be free under any imperial occupation, whether Washington's or Moscow's. The call for workers' councils, coupled with the demand for withdrawal of all occupying armies, formed a coherent revolutionary position.

The Lambertists cite the democratization language without this context. They present one element of the position while omitting the troop withdrawal demand. This allows them to paint the Fourth International as capitulating to Soviet interests. The selective citation works rhetorically because readers don't have access to the full declaration. The technique is classic sectarian dishonesty: not outright lying, but context stripping; presenting part of a position as the whole of it.

The Real Disagreement (Now Visible)

Once you establish that the Lambertist factual claim is wrong, the genuine political debate becomes clear. The actual disagreement wasn't about whether to demand Soviet troop withdrawal. It was about what the uprising meant and what Stalinism represented.

The Lambertists interpreted the Berlin uprising as proof that Stalinism was purely counter-revolutionary and lacked elements of bureaucratic centrism. This vindicated their position: the bureaucracy cannot be pressured leftward. The uprising showed workers rebelling against the Stalinist apparatus itself. This was the political revolution predicted by Trotskyist theory, evidence that bureaucratic regimes could not reform themselves.

The IS read the same events differently. For them, the uprising indicated bureaucratic instability and the potential for mass pressure to shift the regime's direction. Stalin's death in March 1953 had destabilized the ruling caste; the Berlin revolt was evidence that contradiction was opening. The bureaucracy might be pressured into progressive action or overthrown. This was core to the controversial thesis of a central IS member, Michel Pablo: the "march toward socialism" was irreversible; the bureaucracy could be obliged to give certain revolutionary impulses under mass pressure.

Ernest Mandel, also a member of the IS, disputed the fundamental political implications and subsequent strategic consequences derived from Pablo's thesis, particularly as they related to the bureaucracy's potential for self-reform and the liquidation of the revolutionary party. These differences grew during the 1950s. For example, Mandel and the majority of the Fourth International (FI) explicitly rejected Pablo's growing optimism and support for the

Khrushchevite current in the USSR, which suggested the possibility of the bureaucracy undergoing self-reform. The International Secretariat, with Mandel's support, analyzed the post-Stalin reforms as measures of self-defense undertaken by the bureaucracy to preserve its domination, not evidence of a genuine leftward shift. Mandel insisted that bureaucratic degeneration is not the law of socialist revolutions, but the result of defeat and isolation.

So, these are genuine strategic differences about the class character of Stalinist bureaucracies, about whether or when workers' councils or reformed communist parties could lead political revolution, about the historical trajectory of the Soviet regime. Comrades could debate these coherently. The disagreement concerned the nature of Stalinism and the strategy required to overcome it.

But the Lambertist accusation about troop withdrawal isn't part of this debate. It's a factual misrepresentation used to short-circuit genuine engagement.

The Organizational Intelligence: How Sectarian Dishonesty Works

This pattern reveals something important about how organized tendencies conduct polemic. They construct what might be called "straw positions": selective citations and context-stripped formulations designed to be indefensible. They demolish these fabricated positions and declare victory. The actual position held by opponents remains unrefuted because it was never fairly presented.

The technique has several advantages for a tendency.

1. First, it requires less work than genuine engagement. Refuting someone's actual position demands understanding it fully; constructing a strawman is faster.
2. Second, it allows for maximum rhetorical advantage. You can make the opponent look worse by misrepresenting them than by honestly engaging their argument.
3. Third, it enables tendencies to avoid difficult questions their own positions cannot answer. If you misstate what your opponents said, you don't have to address why their actual argument challenges yours.

This isn't unique to Trotskyism. Left organizations across the spectrum deploy this tactic. It's a recurring pathology of sectarian practice.

Why This Matters for Contemporary Organizers

You might ask: why does something from 1953 matter today? The answer is practical. When you're evaluating which left organization to work with, you need to assess their intellectual honesty. Do they fairly represent positions they disagree with? Do they engage opponents' actual arguments or construct strawmen? Do they acknowledge legitimate insights from competing tendencies, or do they only attack?

Organizations that engage dishonestly in polemics often organize dishonestly in other contexts. They present selective information to members about internal debates. They misrepresent opponents' positions in public arguments. They construct narratives designed to persuade rather than to illuminate. Over time, this undermines the organization's ability to learn from experience and develop effective strategy.

The Lambert current's persistent misrepresentation of the 1953 IS position on Berlin is not an isolated incident. It reflects a pattern of selective citation and context-stripping that characterizes their polemics against Pabloism. Once you notice it, you see it everywhere: claims presented without full context, quotes stripped of surrounding argument, positions attributed to opponents that no one actually held.

This matters because the left needs comrades who can discern genuine disagreement from manufactured conflict. We need organizations that engage opponents' actual positions because honest debate is the only way to develop better strategy. Revolutionary movements require rigor. They require the ability to distinguish real political differences from sectarian misrepresentations.

The Strategic Lesson

The IS position on the 1953 Berlin uprising was politically coherent: support the workers' rebellion, call for workers' councils to replace the bureaucratic apparatus, demand withdrawal of all occupying armies. This was a revolutionary position. Whether you agree with Pabloism's assessment of the bureaucracy's potential is a separate question. The position itself was not capitulation; it was not accommodation to Soviet interests.

The Lambertist critique of Pabloism had legitimate force on other grounds: Pablo's theory of bureaucratic self-reform, his strategy of entrism into Stalinist parties, his relative confidence in the bureaucracy's potential to shift leftward. These were real political disagreements worth fighting out. The split that formalized in November 1953 reflected genuine strategic difference about how to build revolutionary organizations in a Stalinist-dominated world.

But the claim about 1953 Berlin was dishonest. It misrepresented the record to make a polemic point.

For organizers, the lesson is clear: when you're reading left critiques of each other, ask the hard questions. Is this the opponent's actual position, or a misrepresentation? Is context being stripped to make something look worse than it is? Are there legitimate insights in the position being attacked, even if you ultimately disagree? Do the critics acknowledge what their opponents got right before explaining what they got wrong?

These questions matter because the left's effectiveness depends on our ability to learn from experience, to correct errors, and to build unity on the basis of honest engagement rather than sectarian dishonesty. The organizations that do this best survive and develop. Those that don't eventually collapse under the weight of accumulated misrepresentations and internal dishonesty.

The 1953 Berlin uprising was a genuine test of revolutionary positions. But it wasn't a test of whether the IS called for Soviet troop withdrawal. They did. It was a test of how the left understood Stalinism and what strategy could overcome it. That's the debate that mattered then. Understanding how that debate was conducted—and how it was distorted—teaches us something essential about building organizations capable of genuine strategic development.